Sophistication Is Overrated

Sophistication Is Overrated

The Slageter Sisters
Babs Horner & Susan Palma

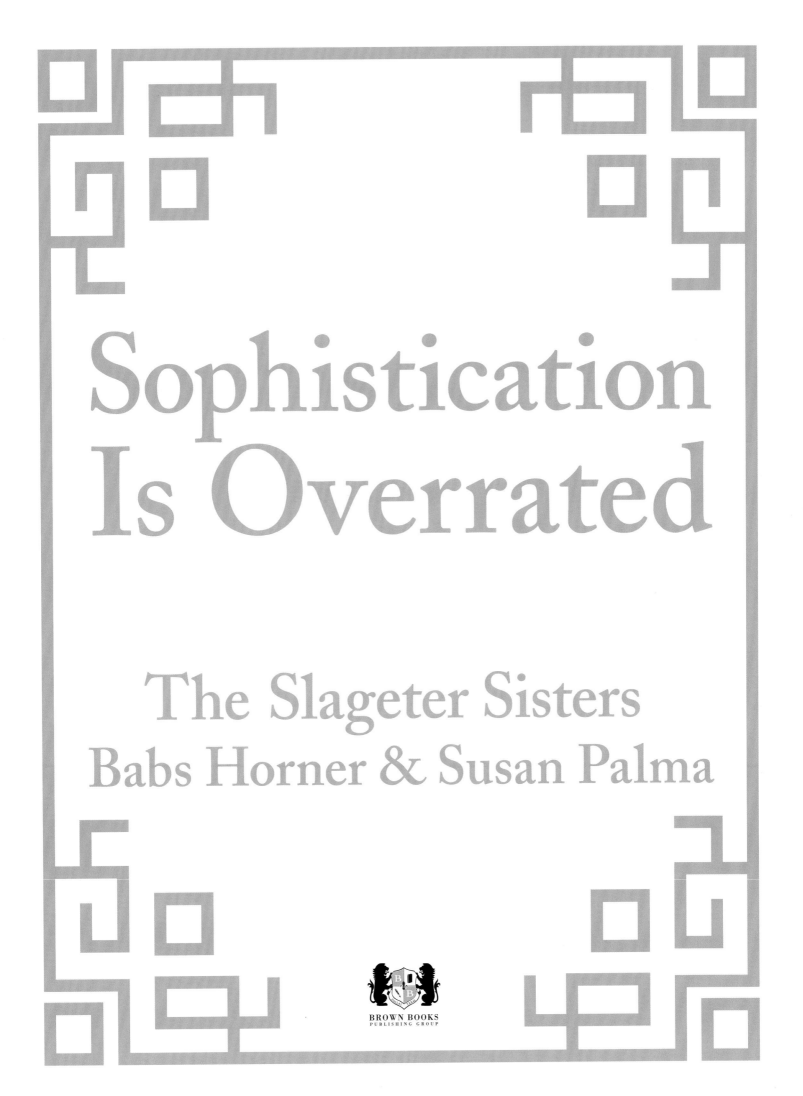

BROWN BOOKS
PUBLISHING GROUP

Sophistication Is Overrated

Brown Books Publishing Group
16250 Knoll Trail Drive, Suite 205
Dallas, Texas 75248
www.BrownBooks.com
(972) 381-0009

A New Era in Publishing™

ISBN 978-1-61254-216-4
LCCN 2015934209

Printed in the United States
10 9 8 7 6 5 4 3 2

For more information or to contact the authors, please go to www.SophisticationIsOverrated.com

We would like to dedicate this book to our parents,
Artsie and Patsy Slageter, who taught us through
example how to belly laugh and have daily
gratitude for the simplest things in life.

Blessed is he who has learned to laugh at himself,
for he shall never cease to be entertained.
—JOHN POWELL

CONTENTS

CONTENTS

So Slageter
CONTENTS

NOTE TO THE READER

*J*ust like a mullet hairdo, this book is business in the front (So Chic) and party in the back (So Slageter). If you dislike shenanigans, many involving cardboard cut-out celebrities or costumed blow-up dolls, be forewarned; only read the So Chic way. Our book is a collaborative effort although there are sections where one of us—either Babs or Sue Sue—does the actual writing, and we refer to ourselves in the first person. If this occurs in the recipe section, that's Babs doing the talking. If you see an "I" in the chapter introductions or the Sisters' Scoop sections, then it's Sue Sue.

ACKNOWLEDGMENTS

We are lucky to have so many people to thank and acknowledge for their help and encouragement. The ironic part is that even though *Sophistication Is Overrated* is our title, all of our friends and supporters are ultra-sophisticated. We have received immeasurable encouragement from Neiman Marcus, Krause Advertising, A Different Perspective, Dallas Design Center, Muffin Lemak (our "best agent"), many high-end gift stores, popular bloggers, and, of course, our many friends. These individuals have been both our ambassadors and our cheerleaders. We could not have had a better photographer. Tom McGovern was game for all of our unconventional themes and even worked long hours in New York and Dallas to highlight our crazy tables. We also thank our buddies, Ann and Ed Kennedy (the Kennedys of Dallas), as well as Luther Menke (Village Garden), all of whom reluctantly answered our pleas to appear in the book (they are the May/December guests in the "Anniversary" section).

A hearty "Thank You" also goes out to the entire team at the Brown Books Publishing Group for their expertise in the book's editing and design. Unfortunately, we do not have the space here to list everyone who helped us with this book. Such recognition could fill several pages, and we would still worry that we had left out key people. Please know that we love you all and that Babs will be bringing each and every one of you one-hundred-and-fifty monogrammed cookies during the holidays.

We also thank our families. This includes our good-natured and loving husbands, Gene and Jack, for years of reluctantly donning boas and mullet wigs because we said, "Trust us, you will have more fun!" Also the Horner sisters, Katsie Turkington and Susie Horner, for being the fresh faces in many of our chapters, not to mention putting up with our countless input about every detail, such as, "We know it's Christmas Eve, but you have to stay up till 3:00 a.m. to crop these pictures." A shout-out to the Palma brothers, Alex and Charlie, for taste- and cook-testing recipes, for wearing outlandish costumes (Elvis and the latte!), and for patiently answering innumerable times questions such as "How do I send this as a Word doc?"

We love you all.

INTRODUCTION

We are the Slageter sisters. Now we know that you are probably saying, "What?! Could you please say that again?" Just say it phonetically: Slā·get·er (long "a"). This was our mantra every time that we introduced ourselves when we were younger. It's true that we both got married just to avoid that whole exercise. So we were tossing around a million titles for our approach, but we always came back to our maiden name because every time we say it, people laugh. And as you will learn, making people laugh is often our Number One goal in life.

We are Babs and Susan—otherwise known as Sue Sue—two sisters who grew up in a unique and entertaining (by all definitions) family. As adult women, we have always lived thousands of miles apart, but we are best friends and talk at least once daily. We both have lived in a number of different cities, stayed connected with friends, and wreaked havoc along the way. For Babs, those cities are Cleveland, Grosse Pointe, London, and New Canaan, and for Sue Sue, it's New Orleans, Houston, Philadelphia, San Francisco, and Dallas. However, it all started in the Midwest, in Cincinnati. Think about that—at five years old we had to spell both Slageter and Cincinnati.

Now that you know we are smart and know how to spell, let us reveal more about ourselves. Babs is the cook who will demonstrate how to prepare—often prepare ahead of time—rave-reviewed recipes. These are all extremely frugal with the butter, and as for mayo, "Stop it!" (our slang for no way).

Sue Sue is the decorator who will show readers how to set a memorable table with items from their own cabinets, stored beneath the stairs, or from thrift, party, and discount stores. Oh, and all of the flowers in this book are purposely purchased from a grocery store. Some of our good friends are talented florists, but just in case readers want to do it effortlessly and affordably on their own, here's how.

Our philosophy for entertaining family and friends has always been the following: We believe that serious sophistication is entirely overrated. Entertaining can be simultaneously beautiful *and* funny. We all need to laugh more.

Now you are probably wondering, *What's wrong with these two?* Good point, but you see, we had no choice. We are this way because of them, as in Artsie and Patsy, our parents; Elizabeth Flynn, a.k.a. Beam (nicknamed because of her sunny disposition), our five-foot Irish grandmother who lived with us; and Margie, Mom's twin. Throughout this book, you will find many recipes and scenarios attributed to these four pillars of our lives.

Our upbringing was a perfect combination of humor and refinement. It was the idyllic *Wonder Years . . .* the Catholic version, complete with saddle shoes and Sister Redempta at the helm. We thought we were rich because we had a new air-conditioned car with the biggest fins, abundant lilac hedges, and Mom's

rose garden to supply the pickle jar vases on our annual May altar in our shared bedroom. Every Saturday, while Artsie played golf, Patsy took her bedecked girls to lunch at the downtown Tea Room. Afterwards, we would go on buying escapades in the finest shops of the Midwest, including Gidding-Jenny, Henry Harris, and Pogue's. Patsy (a former in-store model) was always upfront with her many purchases and showed Artsie all the price tags when she got home. We're not sure if he knew, and he certainly never let on that he did, but Patsy always applied her blue pen to the tags, before she showed them to Artsie, marking all as on sale. What really made us howl is when some items were marked down twice. For this second markdown, Patsy used her red pen. Consequently, the three of us were regularly indulged.

We Slageter sisters always had to be well dressed as we were the kitchen help at every party. For the first hour, passing around hors d'oeuvres on silver trays was our responsibility. We would then skedaddle to the stairway and eavesdrop on the party games, filled with a cacophony of clinking glasses and laughter. Delivering bootleg liquor to the Irish Setter upstairs (as Artsie referred to our grandmother, Beam) was our on-the-steps duty. We learned early the value of a good whiskey sour to get the party rolling as well as a way to mask the mishap of a late-start dinner. In addition, these pilfered libations were our secret weapon for keeping Beam from making us go to bed. Nor did she tell on us for eating the bourbon-soaked red cherries from relinquished glasses or about our favorite activity of rolling around in the guests' furs that were languishing on our parents' double bed. By the way, we particularly coveted Mrs. Lagaly's full-length sheared beaver coat.

Equally important to party entertainment, in Artsie's view, was a costume or, at the very least, a good prop. When being introduced to unsuspecting friends, he would frequently sport his Bubba teeth, a fake handlebar mustache, or perhaps just one of his crazy action hats. He was not immune from donning a whole ensemble, such as appearing as a ballerina or geisha girl at whim. You just never knew what or when—prom night . . . No! As kids, we were both initially embarrassed by Dad's antics, but as the years passed, we noticed that everyone was always laughing and happy whenever Artsie held court. Today, in all honesty, our children are embarrassed by us, and we hope that their children will be embarrassed by them as well. After all, it's a family tradition.

We learned early in our lives that faith, a sense of humor, family, and friends pull you through the unexplainable. During many of our teenage years, Artsie was on dialysis, and he was later a recipient of an early kidney transplant. Even during those trying times, the parties did not stop. There was the Send Off to the Boston Hospital party, the Welcome to the Slageter Hospital Ward party, not to mention the following themed get-togethers: Let's all Dress as Nurses, Candy Stripers, Nuns (all men), and Clowns. Growing up this way, we learned that life may be bleak and that gatherings may not always be jubilant but that you can persevere through most anything if you have humor and friendship.

Our goal in writing this book is to share our thirty-plus years each of expertise, present our delicious—and, yes, healthful—family recipes, reenact some of our parents' favorite party themes (while adding a few timely themes of our own), and, especially, emphasize the fun of helping people relax and enjoy themselves . . . all the while laughing in the process.

Our main purpose, of course, is to honor Artsie, Patsy, and Beam, who are laughing out loud right now in heaven.

TABLE
1

THIRTIETH ANNIVERSARY, WEDDED BLISS

So Chic

A successful marriage requires falling in love many times, always with the same person.

—**MIGNON McLAUGHLIN**

A good marriage would be between a blind wife and a deaf husband.

—**MICHEL DE MONTAIGNE**

By all means marry. If you get a good wife, you'll be happy; if you get a bad one, you'll become a philosopher.

—**SOCRATES**

There are three faithful friends: an old wife, an old dog, and ready money.

—**BENJAMIN FRANKLIN**

Marriage is the alliance of two people, one of whom never remembers birthdays and the other who never forgets them.

—**OGDEN NASH**

I think one reason for a successful marriage is laughter. I think laughter gets you through the rough moments in a marriage.

—**BOB NEWHART**

I have learned that only two things are necessary to keep one's wife happy. First let her think she's having her own way. And second, let her have it.

—**LYNDON B. JOHNSON**

The most important four words for a successful marriage: "I'll do the dishes."

—**ANONYMOUS**

Our pediatrician was rushing out of our wellness checkup appointment. The doctor was apologizing for the rush, but he had to hurry home to surprise his wife with a dinner party for their thirtieth wedding anniversary. I was blindsided when he asked, "How did you celebrate your last anniversary?" Offhandedly I responded, "I think we were all at some pizza emporium immersed in a germ-infested plastic ball area, and we just forgot about it." Then he lambasted me, explaining that in this crazy, disposable society, being happily married is a rarity. He went on to say that we all need to appreciate our spouses and commemorate this most worthy achievement. (Or maybe he was agitated because we were making him really late for his dinner party.)

Upon relating this story to my husband, he responded, "These have been the happiest ten years of my life." Wait. At the time, we'd been married for eighteen years!

Admittedly, since our doctor's spiel, not every one of our anniversaries has been exalted, but at least now we always tell each other "Happy Anniversary!" and we really do observe the big ones.

Our parents were a great example of marital bliss, and luckily both of the Slageter sisters have stayed married, enjoying peaks and weathering the valleys. So if you are fortunate enough to be in a peak year, set the table with those dusty wedding gifts, prepare Babs's delicious dinner, grab a bottle of wine, and celebrate your fortitude.

- Your own dining room may be welcoming, but if you want to shake things up a bit, move a table in front of a fireplace, outdoors, or into the living room.

- If celebrating with company, rent a sixty-inch round table, chairs, and tablecloth (even the dishes and glassware if you choose) from your local party rental company. The next day, when they pick up everything, instant cleanup.

- Keep watching for sales online and at favorite stores for good deals on beautiful dinnerware. These aqua milk glass plates were on sale from Crate & Barrel.

- We love trays. There are so many to choose from: glass, Lucite, tortoise, silver, wood, and even marble ones look great amassed with candlesticks and flowers. Great tray choices can be found at Neiman Marcus and at high-end gift stores such as our Dallas favorites: Forty Five Ten, Madison, St. Michael's Woman's Exchange, Nest, Stanley Korshak, and Ellis-Hill. Browse these Dallas stores online, and then find similar ones in your neck of the woods. In New Canaan, we like The Whitney Shop.

- Popular stores such as West Elm and Z Gallerie have copious tray inventory.

- Make sure that you buy roses a few days early so that they have a chance to open. If the buds are too tight, blow them with a hairdryer for a few seconds. Also, we feel very strongly about only using real flowers. There is no excuse to use fake ones, no matter how real they appear to you. It's gotten so easy to add fresh flowers in the grocery cart along with the eggs.

- If you don't have every item you need, borrow from a friend.

- Beaded napkin rings are from Pier 1 Imports.

- While you are in Pier 1, stock up on votive candles. At a party, every surface deserves a little sparkle.

- Rhinestone picture frames used for name tags are from Two's Company or available at gift and party stores.

- Rethink all objects. These mirrored vases, a craft store find, were actually meant to be pedestals for display. However, turned upside down, they became vases. Really examine objects for multi-purpose possibilities.

- L'Objet pagoda salt and pepper shakers are available from Neiman Marcus.

- Try putting pink light bulbs in lamps for a subtle, romantic glow.

- White roses are a favorite because they are readily available, can stand alone, or look great with any other flower. Here we paired them with lavender hyacinths, all from the grocery store.

Menu

VEGGIE SOUP

BAKED SALMON

PASTA PUTTANESCA

FRESH SAUTÉED SPINACH

CHOCOLATE MOUSSE
WITH WHIPPED CREAM

VEGGIE SOUP

Whether it's your first anniversary or your thirtieth, here's a tasty way to start the festivities.

1 baking potato, peeled and diced

2 carrots, peeled and diced

2 celery ribs, diced

1 onion, small, diced

2 tablespoons butter

32 ounces chicken broth

¼ teaspoon cayenne pepper

1½ cups skim milk

In a soup pot, bring all ingredients to a boil. Lower heat and cook for 1 hour. Cool and puree. Heat soup and stir in 1½ cups skim milk.

Serves 6

BAKED SALMON

You plan on putting a beautiful salmon on the grill, but an unexpected downpour puts an end to that idea and you desperately need an alternative. This recipe is truly the next best thing to grilled salmon.

2 pounds salmon fillet, skin removed

1 lemon, juiced

Seasoned salt, such as Jane's Krazy Salt

2 lemons, sliced thinly (watch your fingers)

Preheat oven to 375 degrees. Place salmon on a foil-lined baking sheet and sprinkle with lemon juice and seasoned salt. Place the sliced lemon around the salmon. Bake for 20 minutes. Remove the salmon to a platter with warmed lemons surrounding the salmon and serve.

Serves 6

PASTA PUTTANESCA

This is one of the most delicious pasta recipes you will ever find. Forget the origins of the name and party on. Then again, if you are throwing the anniversary party for a trophy wife, keep the thought to yourself and chuckle.

2 tablespoons olive oil

1 small onion, chopped

3 garlic cloves, chopped

1 tin anchovies, drained

⅛ cup capers, drained

1 8-ounce jar black olives, drained, cut in halves

½ pint cherry tomatoes, cut in halves

1 8-ounce can tomato sauce

½ pound fettuccini, cooked and drained

Fresh basil, for garnish

Heat the oil in a skillet and add the onion and garlic. Cook until soft. Add the anchovies, capers, olives, tomatoes, and tomato sauce. Cook 15 minutes. Serve over the fettuccini. Garnish with basil.

Serves 6

FRESH SAUTÉED SPINACH

Here's a quick and easy recipe that goes well with many entrees and also adds a bit of color.

1 tablespoon olive oil

1 small onion, chopped

18 ounces fresh spinach (can use 3 6-ounce bags)

¼ teaspoon salt

½ teaspoon ground black pepper

½ teaspoon nutmeg

Heat oil in a large pot with a lid. Add the onion and cook until light brown. Add the spinach. Add salt, pepper, and nutmeg. *Do not stir.* Cover with lid and cook for 8 minutes over medium heat.

Serves 6

CHOCOLATE MOUSSE WITH WHIPPED CREAM

Everybody loves chocolate on that special occasion.

1 12-ounce bag semi-sweet chocolate chips

1 cup half-and-half

4 tablespoons Kahlúa, optional

4 eggs, separated

¼ teaspoon cream of tartar

1 pint whipping cream

1 tablespoon powdered sugar

Combine chocolate chips, half-and-half, and Kahlúa. Cook over low heat until chips are melted. Whisk in egg yolks one at a time until blended. Remove from heat and cool. Beat egg whites with cream of tartar until stiff. Fold the whites into the cooled chocolate mixture. Refrigerate at least 12 hours. Whip the whipping cream with the powdered sugar. Spoon the mousse into pretty glasses—martini glasses add a little extra splash—and top with whipped cream. Sift more powdered sugar over the top. (Note, powdered sugar over desserts, pies, and brownies makes the final presentation so much prettier.)

Serves 6

TABLE
1

FIRST ANNIVERSARY WITH THE
NEW TROPHY WIFE

So Slageter

I'd marry again if I found a man who had fifteen million dollars, would sign over half to me, and guarantee that he would be dead within a year.
—**BETTE DAVIS**

I haven't reported my missing credit card to the police because whoever stole it is spending less than my wife.
—**ILIE NASTASE**

Always get married in the morning. That way if it doesn't work out, you haven't wasted a whole day.
—**MICKEY ROONEY**

I don't think my wife likes me very much. When I had a heart attack, she wrote for an ambulance.
—**FRANK CARSON**

I was married by a judge. I should have asked for a jury.
—**GROUCHO MARX**

There's nothing like a good cheating song to make me run home to my wife.
—**STEVEN CURTIS CHAPMAN**

I haven't talked to my wife in years. I don't want to interrupt her.
—**RODNEY DANGERFIELD**

When a man opens a car door for his wife, it's either a new car or a new wife.
—**PRINCE PHILIP**

So Slaqeter
THE INSPIRATION

We had just moved from California to Texas and were surprised and elated when a beautiful invitation arrived in the mailbox. A thoughtful neighbor, whom we had yet to meet, decided to include us at a garden soiree on a gorgeous spring evening. When we arrived, the elegant cocktail party was in full swing: swishing skirts, towering stilettos, dashing blazers, wine flowing, and hors d'oeuvre trays circling. But wait. What's that blur? A dog? Oh my goodness, no, it's a three-year-old child, darting precariously under bridges of adult legs and being chased by his harried grandfather.

As Good Samaritans and experienced catchers, we grabbed the screeching ankle biter and returned him to his exasperated charge. During our disjointed conversation, Gramps dropped the bombshell: "Be quiet, son, and let Daddy talk." I have to say, our reactions were Oscar-worthy. Just as we were trying to digest this new information, in struts the mama, who turned out to be a blonde bombshell who looked to be about twenty-eight years old. She then gave the order, "Daddy, go on and get Rainbow home 'cause I am taking the girls and the limo to karaoke night and will see you *mañana*!"

I could not even look at my hubby, as I knew that if we made eye contact we would end up doubled over and guffawing on the floor. We saved that for the walk home, but we stayed for just one more 9:00 nightcap with Daddy and child.

- Centerpiece silver trophy was bought at an antique store many years ago in anticipation of a trophy wife party. Ta-da! Keep your eyes peeled for unusual finds to plan a theme around.

- The gold bust trophies were borrowed from our friend, Jane, who won these . . . not for what you are thinking, but for artistic achievement. You never know what your friends have hidden away.

- All other gold (or plastic) trophies in various sizes can be purchased from any party store or from Oriental Trading for about $1 each. Filled with beautiful flowers, anything looks good.

- Use your kids' sports trophies, and ask your friends if you can borrow their kids' trophies as well. More is better in this case. Who doesn't want to find another use for these things?

- The trophies are good to use as place cards as well. See who can find their intended seat with trophies marked with "Best Botox," "Best Practical Joker," "Funniest Stories," and "Most Likely to Stay till 2 a.m." All in good fun, of course.

- Reading glasses are collected from every room in the house, or if you are under forty-five, buy in bulk from Costco or find darling ones from eyebobs.

- The "Miss America" homemade banner draped on a chair is another great theme for a whole separate party. Name your friends "Miss Chievous," "Miss Understood," "Miss Begotten," "Miss Informed" . . . and the list goes on.

- Buy a stuffed Chihuahua. You will use repeatedly. A wardrobe staple to carry in your purse, like many trophy wives.

- You can get giant jewels by the box from party stores.

- The wheelchair for the "Great Catch"—a one-hundred-year-old, really rich hubby—was rented for the day at the pharmacy.

- The oxygen for the really rich hubby is a child's discarded asthma nebulizer.

- Baby paraphernalia was borrowed from our friend, Robyn, who is a new grandmother. She had rooms full of this stuff.

- As we explained in the introduction, we love the blow-up doll friend. We dress her (or him) up for most of our events. We do order online but only on eBay. You will understand this directive if you ever google "plastic doll" by mistake. Trust us on this one; don't! And it should be obvious which ones we buy.

- We collect magnifying glasses from all over the world (most were bought in London and Paris markets). We thought this table was a good theme to incorporate this eye-opening collection.

- The First Anniversary cake topper was made to our specifications at our local grocery store bakery.

- Of course, we had to make a run to the drugstore for essential ninety-year-old groom aids.

REAL
TROPHY
WIVES
IN THE
WILD

TABLE
2

I'D RATHER BE IN PARIS!

So Chic

When good Americans die, they go to Paris.
—OSCAR WILDE

Lunch kills half of Paris, supper the other half.
—CHARLES DE MONTESQUIEU

I'd like to see Paris before I die. Philadelphia will do.
—MAE WEST

Cities have sexes: London is a man, Paris a woman, and New York a well-adjusted transexual.
—ANGELA CARTER

I love Paris in the summer when it sizzles.
—COLE PORTER

If *Sex in the City* taught us anything, it's that Paris is the only city in the world that New Yorkers actually fantasize about.
—ELIZABETH BARD

CLARK GRISWOLD: There's the Left Bank, kids. I'll bet you can't guess what bank is on the right.
RUSS GRISWOLD: The Bank of America?

No one said finding Paris would be easy; I only said it would be worth it.
—CON TEMPLATE

15

ur families have had many memorable Griswold-style European family vacations (as in the eight-person entourage although, sadly, minus Chevy Chase and the berets). This section is not actually about our beloved Paris, per se. Rather, it *is* about our French collections of Hermès scarves, Limoges boxes, and Old Paris porcelain, which we have unearthed from nooks and crannies worldwide. Oh, the thrill of the find.

Back in the day, after the tooth fairy awarded the anticipated coinage under our pillows, each of our baby teeth magically re-appeared in the Limoges boxes inscribed *dents au lait* (milk teeth) that were interspersed in the collection on our parents' dresser. Keeping with Patsy's gift-giving tradition, my box was pink and Babs's was blue.

Another stellar reason to start a collection of your favorite items is to ease the gift-giving burdens that seem to befall men. Have you ever received that perfume box as large as a coffee table? The lone item left mid-aisle in a department store that beckons guys on Christmas Eve at 3:00 p.m.? Me too. To alleviate such memorable gifts, start a collection and let your gentlemen know. This is easier for everybody on Christmas as well as Mother's Day and your birthday. As a result of this brilliant tactic, my charm bracelet is crowded—I'm loving the football helmet one, really—the Limoges box tray is overflowing, and my arm is starting to look tribal because of a plethora of enamel bracelets. But wait, the presents can't be expensive every time, so we should also covet books, ornaments, anything fiber optic, funny hats (à la Artsie), singing ("press here") stuffed animals, and any unique gag gift. My favorite gift one Christmas (besides hubby's snow globe charm) was a somewhat beautifully wrapped box that contained a soiled knife and fork, which I later learned represented one son taking me out to dinner and the other pledging for the two of us to make dinner together. So let's add those thoughtful gifts to a collection of memories, which trumps all aforementioned collections. (Say it all together now: "Awwwww!")

- For this table, we let our collections take center stage. We used every piece of our white Paris porcelain down the table's center. This has been amassed for twenty years, but you could use any white bowls and compotes for a similar effect. Look for white and gold compotes in antique stores and china departments of high-end stores as well as website such as Amazon, Etsy, and The Find.

- The Cartier-like rolling napkin rings are from Crate & Barrel. Many stores that sell place settings and silverware stock a large selection of napkin rings.

- Look for linen placemats to dress your table. These were a present from a friend who gave them as a gift four at a time on three different birthdays. Linens and tableware are perfect presents for a frequent hostess. Some great mats can be found at Neiman Marcus, Horchow, Madison, Ellis-Hill, and Anthropologie, to name just a few stores.

- Since our mother always said that a displayed bowl must be filled or put away, we used a combination of blue hydrangea and lemons to fill our containers.

- We always look for silver wine coasters at antique and gift stores, as we like to place two to four on the table for easy access to the fruit of the vine. It just looks more refined than a plain bottle.

- The white-and-gold water glasses from Forty Five Ten were also a gift from a friend who gave these to me in pairs. They also double as vases.

- Take those scarves (maybe a few Hermès) out of their tissued boxes in the back of your drawer and adorn each chair back.

- This is a perfect time to showcase your French collections, such as Limoges boxes, on a beautiful tray. The Cottage Shop has many one-of-a-kind Limoges boxes.

Menu

MINI CREPES

BISTRO SALAD

FILET MIGNON STEAK

SCALLOPED POTATOES

MACAROONS

LEMON
MERINGUE PIE

RECIPES

MINI CREPES

These are appetizer size and should be prepared ahead of time. Leave the baking until the end in order to serve them warm.

CREPE MIXTURE
½ cup water
½ cup whole milk
2 eggs
½ teaspoon salt
1 cup flour
2 tablespoons butter, melted

Mix all ingredients and refrigerate for 2 hours. Lightly spray a non-stick frying pan with PAM. Heat the pan to medium-high heat. Add 1 heaping tablespoon of the crepe mixture to the pan. Spread into a 4-inch circle. Cook for 30 seconds and then flip and cook for another 30 seconds. Remove and set aside. Repeat until you use the entire mixture.

FILLINGS
Any of the following including combinations to taste:

Fresh spinach leaves with stems removed
Ham
Gruyère cheese
Brie cheese

Fill and roll the crepes ahead of time. Bake at 350 degrees for 5 minutes and serve.

Makes 18 small crepes

BISTRO SALAD

Takes seconds; tastes delicious and fresh.

2 heads Bibb lettuce
½ to 1 cup blue cheese, crumbled

TARRAGON DRESSING
3 tablespoons white wine vinegar
¼ cup olive oil
1 teaspoon salt
1 teaspoon honey
¼ cup fresh tarragon leaves, chopped

Mix all dressing ingredients and toss with the salad.

Serves 6

SCALLOPED POTATOES

Wonderful, rich-tasting potatoes. All you do is slice them, layer them, and bake them.

4 large baking potatoes
Salt
Ground black pepper
½ pound Gruyère cheese, shredded
1¼ cups chicken broth
1¼ cups light cream

Slice the potatoes very thin; use a mandolin if available. Place a layer of potatoes in a 9x13-inch casserole dish. Salt and pepper the potato slices and sprinkle with cheese. Repeat this process, adding 2 more layers. Mix the broth and cream and pour over the potatoes. For a nice bit of added color, sprinkle the top with paprika. Bake at 375 degrees for 1 hour. Let stand for 15 minutes before serving.

Serves 6

FILET MIGNON STEAK

On pleasant evenings, we enjoy grilling the steaks outside. However, when the weather or the mood forces you inside, there is a great way to cook the steaks in an iron or heavy skillet.

6 filet mignon steaks, 1½ to 2 inches thick

BABS'S SPECIAL RUB

3 tablespoons instant beef bouillon

1 teaspoon paprika

1 teaspoon onion powder

1 teaspoon garlic powder

1 teaspoon ground black pepper

Mix the bouillon, paprika, onion powder, garlic powder, and pepper in a small bowl. Rub the mixture on both sides of each steak. Let the steaks sit at room temperature for 1 hour.

GRILL

Over a high heat, cook the steaks for 5 minutes per side for medium rare.

IRON SKILLET

Heat 2 tablespoons olive oil in a skillet. Over a high heat, cook the steaks for 5 minutes per side for medium rare. Remove the steaks and place on a covered platter. Lower the heat to medium and add ¼ cup beef broth and ¼ cup red wine to the skillet, scraping the skillet with a metal spatula. Pour over the steaks. You can add a little extra zest by topping each steak with a tablespoon of blue cheese. Absolutely rich tasting and delicious.

Serves 6

(It's not likely, but just in case you have some leftover steak, slice it thinly and serve over fresh greens with tarragon dressing for a terrific salad for lunch tomorrow.)

LEMON MERINGUE PIE

Delight your guests with this classic balance of sweet and tart. They'll think you took lessons from a chef.

GRAHAM CRACKER CRUST

1 cup graham cracker crumbs

2 tablespoons butter, melted

2 tablespoons sugar

Mix all ingredients. Pat into a pie plate. Bake at 350 degrees for 8 to 10 minutes.

LEMON FILLING

1 cup water

½ cup sugar

2 tablespoons butter

¼ cup cornstarch

¼ cup water

3 eggs, separated (save the whites for
   the meringue)

3 tablespoons lemon rind

¼ cup lemon juice

Combine the water, sugar, and butter in a medium saucepan. Cook on medium heat for 5 minutes. Mix the cornstarch and ¼ cup of water until smooth and then add to the above mixture. Cook over medium heat, whisking until thick. Add the yolks, mixing quickly. Add the rind and juice. Pour into the pie crust. Refrigerate.

MERINGUE

3 egg whites

¼ teaspoon cream of tartar

¼ teaspoon salt

⅔ cup sugar

Beat the egg whites with the cream of tartar and salt until stiff peaks appear. Slowly add sugar, stirring it into the beaten egg whites. Spoon on top of the pie. Bake at 350 degrees for about 10 minutes until the meringue is light brown.

Serves 6

MACAROONS

So yummy.

4 egg whites

1 14-ounce bag Baker's coconut

1 tube pure almond paste, shredded

1 cup powdered sugar

Parchment paper—a must.

Beat the egg whites until you create stiff peaks. Mix all the ingredients together. Line cookie sheets with parchment paper. Spoon the dough onto the parchment paper. Bake at 325 degrees for 16 to 18 minutes.

Makes 30 cookies

TABLE

2

LIVE FROM PARIS, HERE'S JULIA!

So Slageter

People who love to eat
are the best people.
—Julia Child

I was thirty-two when I
started cooking; up until
then I just ate.
—Julia Child

Drama is very
important in life.
You have to come
on with a bang. You
never want to go out with a
whimper. Everything can
have drama if it's done
right, even a pancake.
—Julia Child

A party without cake is
really just a meeting.
—Julia Child

Maybe the cat has
fallen in the stew or the
lettuce has frozen or the
cake has collapsed—
eh bien, tant pis!
—Julia Child

The only time to eat
diet food is while you are
waiting for the steak to cook.
—Julia Child

Always remember,
if you are alone in the
kitchen and you drop the
lamb, you can always just
pick it up. Who's
going to know?
—Julia Child

Everything in
moderation, including
moderation.
—Julia Child

Here's our very own Julia, straight from the Cordon Bleu, buttering up to Babs and our beret-wearing friend, Fifi. A picture is worth a thousand words, right?

- We frequently like to have an unexpected guest (Julia) arrive mid-party to get things hopping. Austin Powers, *Saturday Night Live* characters, Cher, and Bill Clinton have all attended our parties. It's so fun to watch the room buzz. Check out the website of Tapley Entertainment (a company specializing in celebrity lookalikes) to get ideas. If the real lookalike is not in your budget, dress up a friend. Maybe you can even coerce your husband into donning a themed costume. (Then you will always be prepared to have fun at future costume parties and won't dread the thought of it.) Here is our very own Julia and a buttered lobster in a pot at a charity Halloween party.

- In our opinion, nothing contributes to the ambience of a French dinner more than fiber optic Eiffel towers. These were actually a gift from our friend, Claire, who braved security and filled her Birkin bag with these little gems. *Merci, mon amie!* You can find your own Eiffel towers at the Bizrate website.

- Dig in your closet and unearth all things French: berets, baguettes, fake ciggies . . . and where's that poodle?

- Don't forget Fifi (our French blow-up friend) dressed *très chic*. But our most important tip: don't put her next to renowned womanizer lookalikes. Just saying.

- Sometimes we just plop a cardboard replica on the front porch to welcome guests. A strategically placed Austin Powers peeking out from a formal dining room drapery always adds some fun. Peruse the offerings from the company Cardboard Cutouts or the stand ups at Allposters.com. We have found that most of our friends enjoy being greeted by Pamela Anderson and David Hasselhoff or perhaps even getting a glimpse of George Bush 41 skydiving from the tree. If you have a guest of honor or a birthday girl, superimpose her face on a Scarlett O'Hara or Batwoman stand up.

- We have found that men might balk initially, but they end up having the time of their lives while sporting a boa. For all of you naysayers, think of all the *Saturday Night Live* skits and movies that always get rave reviews and belly laughs with stars in drag for a scene or two.

- At a football pep rally at my son's high school, we pleaded with reluctant, burly teachers to be cheerleaders, complete with skirts, lipstick, and wigs. Surprised peals of laughter and standing ovations made school legends out of these neophytes.

- And for some reason, a rubber chicken is usually a crowd-pleaser, regardless of the theme. We love the Archie McPhee website for our chickens.

TABLE
3

YULETIDE BRUNCH

So Chic

Nothing says holidays like a cheese log.
—**ELLEN DEGENERES**

What I don't like about office Christmas parties is looking for a job the next day.
—**PHYLLIS DILLER**

Santa Claus has the right idea: visit people only once a year.
—**VICTOR BORGE**

Christmas is a necessity. There has to be at least one day of the year to remind us that we are here for something else besides ourselves.
—**ERIC SEVAREID**

When did wishing someone a Merry Christmas become politically incorrect?
—**SUZANNE WOODS FISHER**

The perfect Christmas tree? All Christmas trees are perfect.
—**CHARLES BARNARD**

I don't want Christmas season to end because it's the only time I can legitimately indulge in my particular addiction: glitter.
—**ELOISA JAMES**

I once bought my kids a set of batteries for Christmas with a note saying, "Toys not included."
—**BERNARD MANNING**

ince our mother Patsy was such an expert shopper—and there were only two of us children—our tree hovered over an obscene number of Christmas presents. We usually slept in and then feasted on sausage and egg casserole, countless seven-layer bars, and rum balls. (No Paleo Diet menu at the Slageters during the holidays.) Frequently we were lethargic after that smorgasbord, but the true reason for our uncharacteristic patience in opening presents was our foolish, sisterly, deep-dark secret. And since our parents are now in heaven, we can reveal this secret to you. Long before Santa's visit, we would meticulously open, examine, and re-wrap each other's gifts late at night in a clandestine basement closet. Since each of us always received the exact same items, except for the color, obviously we were in no real rush for an early Christmas morning activity. In retrospect, this definitely defeated the purpose, but on the upside, we both became excellent wrappers.

If Dad's holidays were Halloween and Valentine's Day, Mom's was Christmas. She went into overdrive beginning December 1. Back in the '60s there were very few fake trees, so you didn't see signs of Christmas decorating until mid-December, except at our house. The week after Thanksgiving, we would make our pilgrimage to Cappells, a shrine to ribbon, sequins, and glue. This independently owned craft emporium was magical, and we practically lived there every first week of December. We think Patsy was only convinced into serving as our Brownie troop co-leader because of the craft segments. Until Mrs. Slageter, no one had ever seen pink and green ribbon sit-upons. Think Betty Draper on *Mad Men* demonstrating how to glitter a stuffed robin to twenty-four eager eight-year-olds. And then, after a

long drag on her Kent ciggie, she goes AWOL, leaving the cleanup, dues collecting, and Girl Scout cookie talk to her exasperated co-leader.

Sometimes on Christmas day, Mom would use the sequined skirt that she made to go around the tree as a tablecloth and utilize her largest silver tray of cookies to hide the hole. She would then return the skirt to its real home after all the packages were gone. We have now surmised that since she had invested so much time in its creation, she wanted that skirt seen everywhere. Here are Babs's daughters wearing Mom's original and our re-created replica. These are very simple to make with lots of felt, sequins, roping, fringe, and time. (We have found that doing this sewing while binge watching *Downton Abbey*, *Mad Men*, or reruns of *Modern Family* makes us feel better about ourselves because at least we are also doing something productive.)

- In order to bring a little more warmth to the table, we dressed the chair backs with a half yard of red-and-white fabric cut with pinking shears and glued grosgrain ribbon bows to finish.

- To copy our Mom's felt-and-sequin tree skirt or tablecloth: since there are many sites online that explain this process succinctly, we suggest you might want to do a Web search using the words "sequin," "Christmas tree," and "skirts." But if you feel confident to wing it from our picture, here's how:

- Buy two yards of white felt, colored felt, and threads to match from a fabric store. Cut into a large circle with a twenty-four-inch hole for the tree trunk and one slit. Use children's books as a reference to make holiday shapes in many different felt colors. Buy bulk sequins and gold stars from Cartwright's. Before the sequins arrive, it's a good idea to buy at least one sewing box with twenty-four compartments at The Container Store to house these thousands of sparkle pieces. Trust us on this tip. For the gold trim and fringe, we love M&J Trimming. Now grab a friend or start a group, put on some old movies, and let the elves start sewing.

- Our axiom: Tabasco-laden Bloody Marys and cutout cookies always produce a merry Christmas morning.

- We don't take much time for this table since we arrange it in the morning before Midnight Mass on Christmas Eve. We actually forage other parts of the house (from coffee tables, bookshelves, and the tree) for our favorite Christmas items to decorate the table. We love our glittered trees from Scully & Scully as well as our varied Santa collection, especially the German papier-mâché ones from Ino Schaller, found on eBay and Amazon.com. Filled-to-the-brim large glass bowls as well as vases with ornaments and interspersed battery-powered lights add extra festivity and sparkle.

Menu

BLOODY MARYS

EGGS "BENEDICTO"

BAKED ASPARAGUS

POTATO PANCAKES

PECAN ROLLS

BABS'S COOKIES

PECAN ROLLS

These are the real presents from Santa at our house. The stockings can wait . . . head to the kitchen. The pecan rolls are a delicious addition to any brunch or breakfast and just go so well with coffee or breakfast tea.

THE DOUGH

1 package yeast

1 cup scalded milk cooled to lukewarm (110 degrees)

½ cup sugar

1 teaspoon salt

2 eggs, beaten

1 stick butter, melted and cooled to room temperature

4¼ cups flour

Put yeast in a mixing bowl. Add milk and stir. Let rest until dissolved, about 20 minutes. Stir in sugar, salt, and eggs. Add half of the melted butter, and then add half of the flour. Beat until smooth. Add the remaining flour and beat. Add the remaining butter and mix. Knead until smooth. We use the kneading hook on my mixer. Place the dough in a greased bowl, cover, and let rise until doubled in size, about 1 hour. Divide the dough in two. Roll out into 2 rectangles.

FILLING

4 tablespoons butter, softened

½ cup sugar

2 tablespoons cinnamon

Mix the sugar and cinnamon. On each rectangle, evenly spread out 2 tablespoons of the softened butter. Then sprinkle the sugar and cinnamon over the dough. Roll up each rectangle of dough. Set aside.

TOPPING

1 cup butter

1 cup chopped pecans

1 cup brown sugar

4 teaspoons light corn syrup

Mix the ingredients in a saucepan and bring to a boil. Pour evenly into 2 9x13-inch baking dishes. Cut each dough roll into 12 slices, approximately 1" thick. Place 12 slices in each baking dish. Cover and let rise until doubled in size, about 1 hour. Bake at 375 degrees for 25 minutes. Remove from oven. Line a large cookie sheet with non-stick foil. Put the cookie sheet on top of the baking dish and carefully turn over. Presto! The pecan rolls are now on the cookie sheet, topping included.

SUGGESTION FOR THE OVERLY BUSY CHEF: instead of the homemade dough, you can use 1 package Pillsbury hot roll mix. Halve the fillings and topping. Makes 1 9x13-inch pan of pecan rolls.

Makes 24 rolls

BAKED ASPARAGUS

How easy is this? The Parmesan really forms a delicious crust.

24 asparagus spears

Olive oil

Salt

Pepper

Freshly grated Parmesan cheese

Place asparagus on a cookie sheet lined with non-stick foil. Drizzle with oil and sprinkle with salt, pepper, and cheese. Bake at 400 degrees for 15 minutes.

Serves 6

EGGS "BENEDICTO"

Babs's very own Italian version of the classic. Christmas is a very busy time, so take my advice and make the sauce ahead of time. The entire brunch takes less time to prepare than you would think because the cookies are all made well in advance. It's all about being organized.

SAUCE
3 tablespoons canola oil

1 small onion, diced

3 garlic cloves, diced

3 tablespoons flour

½ cup chicken broth

½ cup milk

1 14-ounce can diced tomatoes, drained

2 fresh basil leaves

1 teaspoon salt

1 teaspoon pepper

½ pound smoked mozzarella cheese, sliced

3 sandwich-size English muffins, split

6 eggs

1 tablespoon vinegar

GARNISH
Diced fresh tomatoes

Slivered fresh basil

Heat oil in a saucepan and sauté the onion and garlic. Whisk in the flour and mix well. Add chicken broth and milk; cook until thick. Puree the drained tomatoes, basil leaves, salt, and pepper in a blender. Add the blended mixture to the sauce. Put cheese slices on the muffins. Place on a cookie sheet in a 350-degree oven for about 7 minutes until the cheese is melted. Crack 6 eggs into cups. We use measuring cups. Fill a large pot with water about halfway and bring to a boil. Add 1 tablespoon of vinegar to the water. Slip the eggs gently into the boiling water. Cook 3 minutes. Use a slotted spoon to remove the eggs. Be sure they are drained. Place one on each prepared muffin. Pour warm sauce over the eggs and garnish with the fresh tomatoes and basil.

Serves 6

POTATO PANCAKES

Whether it is brunch or breakfast, potatoes are a mainstay. They complement the eggs and the asparagus. Just think, a well-rounded meal to kick off a great day.

2 large baking potatoes

4 tablespoons bread crumbs

2 tablespoons Parmesan cheese

3 tablespoons finely diced red onion

1 tablespoon finely diced parsley

½ teaspoon salt

½ teaspoon pepper

2 eggs beaten

2 tablespoons canola oil

Shred potatoes. Wrap in a tea towel, squeeze, and drain well. Mix all ingredients and form into 12 pancakes. Heat 2 tablespoons canola oil in a skillet. Cook pancakes over medium heat for 5 minutes on each side until golden brown. If necessary, you can reheat them at 350 degrees for 8 minutes.

BIG TIP OF THE DAY: The potatoes will discolor your tea towels, so unless you are stupendously wealthy or own the towel company, shred the potatoes directly on cheesecloth. Squeeze out the water in the sink and drain well. Throw away the used cheesecloth.

Serves 6

BLOODY MARYS

Wilted celery stalks are out; freshly sliced cucumber stalks are in. They add a new flavor, and the celery salt takes care of that traditional celery craving if there is one. Because of the full flavors, these do well as non-alcoholic versions. We just don't understand that concept.

1 46-ounce can tomato juice

3 tablespoons Worcestershire sauce

¾ teaspoon Tabasco sauce (red)

¼ cup horseradish

Celery salt

Fresh lime or lemon juice

Vodka

1 8-ounce jar of good, green olives soaked in vodka to cover

1 large cucumber cut into thin stalks

Mix the tomato juice, Worcestershire sauce, Tabasco sauce, and horseradish in a pitcher. Sprinkle an ample amount of celery salt on a small plate, wet the edge of each glass with fresh lime or lemon juice, and then turn the wet rim in the celery salt. Pour 1 jigger of vodka into each glass, add ice, pour in the tomato juice mixture, and add 2 olives. Garnish with 1 cucumber stalk.

Serves 4 to 6

SERVING HINT: to avoid diluting the cocktail, refrigerate the glasses and tomato juice mixture ahead of time and spare the ice.

BABS'S COOKIES

These are some of the cookie recipes that are always a favorite of Babs's family, friends, and customers. She would start baking in September to fill the Christmas orders. Unless you are making over 5,000 cookies, you can probably wait until closer to Christmas. Make them, freeze them, thaw them, and serve them.

GINGERBREAD COOKIES

My daughter, Katie, makes two batches to build her annual gingerbread house. Since she has the momentum and the Mixmaster going, she makes additional batches for cookies.

3 cups flour

1 teaspoon baking soda

½ teaspoon salt

2 teaspoons ground ginger

2 teaspoons ground cinnamon

½ teaspoon nutmeg

¾ cup dark brown sugar

¾ cup butter, softened

¼ cup unsulphured molasses

¼ cup honey

1 egg

Mix the flour, baking soda, salt, ginger, cinnamon, and nutmeg in a bowl. Separately mix the sugar and butter, then add molasses, honey, egg, and mix. Add mixtures together. Chill dough for at least 2 hours. On a floured surface using a floured rolling pin, roll out the dough to a thickness of ⅛ inch to ¼ inch. Use cookie cutters to make gingerbread men and your other favorite Christmas shapes. Place cookies on a cookie sheet and bake at 350 degrees for 12 minutes.

Each batch makes 60 cookies

APRICOT DROP COOKIES

½ cup butter

4 tablespoons whipped cream cheese

¼ cup sugar

1 cup flour

1 teaspoon baking powder

½ cup shredded coconut

½ cup apricot preserves

Mix butter, cream cheese, and sugar. Separately mix the flour and baking powder together and add the above mixture. Add coconut and apricot preserves. Use a teaspoon to drop each cookie onto a cookie sheet. Bake at 350 degrees for 15 minutes. Allow to cool.

ICING
1 cup powdered sugar

3 tablespoons water

½ cup apricot preserves

Mix and top the cooled cookies.

Makes 36 cookies

ALMOND COCONUT BARS

¼ cup butter, softened

¼ cup dark brown sugar

¾ cup flour

Mix butter and sugar. Add flour and mix. Press into an 8-inch baking dish. Bake at 350 degrees for 10 minutes. Remove and cool.

FILLING
2 eggs, beaten

½ cup dark brown sugar

1 tablespoon flour

1 cup coconut, shredded

1 cup slivered almonds

Mix together and pour over crust. Bake at 350 degrees for 15 minutes.

Makes 36 bars

COCONUT MINT BARS

6 tablespoons butter

1 square unsweetened chocolate

¼ cup sugar

¾ cup flour

Melt butter and chocolate together in a small saucepan. Stir in sugar and flour. Pat into a 9x13-inch baking dish. Bake at 350 degrees for 10 minutes. Let cool.

TOPPING
1½ cups coconut, shredded

¾ cup chopped pecans

3 tablespoons crème de menthe

1 can (8 ounces) sweetened condensed milk

Mix all ingredients together. Pour on top of cooled crust and bake at 350 degrees for 25 minutes.

THE FINAL TOUCH
1½ cups 60% cocoa bittersweet chocolate chips

While still hot from the oven, top with 1½ cups 60% cocoa bittersweet chocolate chips. Let melt and spread over bars. Let cool and cut into small squares.

Makes 48 bars

BRING ON THE CANDY CANES AND MILK DUDS; THE JUICE FAST AND SPIN CLASSES START ON MONDAY

So Slageter

Whoever thought a tiny candy bar should be called fun size was a moron.

—GLENN BECK

Christmas is like candy: it slowly melts in your mouth sweetening every taste bud, making you wish it could last forever.

—RICHELLE E. GOODRICH

My grandmother started walking five miles a day when she was sixty. She's ninety-seven now, and we don't know where the heck she is.

—ELLEN DEGENERES

Whenever I feel the need to exercise, I lie down until it goes away.

—PAUL TERRY

I believe that every human being has a finite number of heartbeats. I don't intend to waste any of mine running around doing exercises.

—NEIL ARMSTRONG

Squats are a form of torture designed by people who don't need to do squats in the first place.

—NORA ROBERTS

Candy is nature's way of making up for Mondays.

—UNKNOWN

Sometimes I think that the one thing I love most about being an adult is the right to buy candy whenever and wherever I want.

—RYAN GOSLING

O ur tree in the living room (one of three) was different every year, save one characteristic: it was always flocked white. In the era of giant bubbling lights and pine trees laden with three boxes of tinsel, this was definitely a cultural anomaly. In addition, most of the ornaments were handmade and elaborately themed. Sometimes the motif was just a color, other times objects such as angels one year and another year small Nantucket baskets filled with perfectly placed velvet pastel flowers. Our all-time favorite tree had all pink ornaments; even the lights were strands of pink and white roses. We would frequently sneak down in the middle of the night and just stare in awe. We were mesmerized as if the tree was a crackling fire or a Disney movie. But wait. What is that blob of glaring red peeking from the lowest branch? Upon closer inspection, we discovered a ten-inch stuffed Snoopy disguised with a hastily fashioned cotton ball beard and Santa hat, clutching a four-piece box of Whitman candy. Salivating for a potential midnight chocolate fix, we greedily opened the box. To our dismay, we found only empty wrappers and this note: "Ha ha! The Phantom strikes again!" Much to Patsy's chagrin and our disappointment, our dad, Artsie, covertly re-filled and re-emptied Snoopy's stash repeatedly each season. The tacky dog prevailed regardless of the dazzling Bergdorf Goodman window-worthy themed tree. And by the way, that same garish Snoopy continues to hide on a lower branch of our Christmas tree each year. Tradition.

Are you ready to learn another Christmas handicraft in addition to the tree skirt? Ahhhh, finally . . . Candy Land. We actually didn't make these candy trees growing up. About thirteen years ago, these were created with my dynamo decorating partner, Muffin Lemak, for the fabulous Dallas charity event called Kappa Tablescapes. The centerpiece was a five-foot bonbon-laden tree surrounded by ten more candy trees of diverse heights, square candied "presents," and for comic relief, dental floss and toothbrushes. It was such an enjoyable experience and so well received that it's become our holiday tradition ever since. On a side note, for years we were known as decorators / glue gun instructors.

This sweet craft is a striking, easy way to decorate and a fun family project for kids of all ages (bring on the grandparents). Use as a centerpiece for a dining table as well as massed on an entry table or sideboard. We have found that these always elicit compliments, are timeless, and are a lot of bang for the buck. As you can see in the photo, all you need are some Styrofoam cones, lots of drugstore candy, gumballs, glue guns, and of course, our plastic blow-up doll dressed as an elf. But remember, "He sees you when you are EATING, he knows if you've been bad or good, so be good for heaven's sake!"

- Any craft store such as Michaels or Hobby Lobby will have the Styrofoam tree cones and squares for presents. Just remember that in order to cover every inch, you will need more candy and glue than you think. It is frustrating to run out of anything at midnight when you are almost finished.

- Buy double the amount of glue sticks you were planning, as you will go through these quickly. Be sure to get low-heat glue guns.

- Cover your work area with a large piece of oilcloth to protect the table.

- Get candy from any place. Candy kisses, Smarties, large and small gumdrops, orange and spearmint slices, and green and red peppermints work extremely well.

- Always start at the top. It's the perfect spot for a chocolate kiss.

- The trees can actually be re-used for many years. Store in well-sealed plastic bins in a cool area.

- We like to start in the morning when not tempted by that chocolate . . . and in anticipation of Babs's Christmas cookies.

TABLE
4

SISTERS' DINNER

So Chic

Never let an angry sister comb your hair.
—**Patricia McCann**

One sister will lie and the other sister will swear to it.
—**Our Dad**

If your sister is in a tearing hurry to go out and won't catch your eye, she's wearing your best sweater.
—**Pam Brown**

More than Santa Claus, your sister knows when you've been bad or good.
—**Linda Sunshine**

Big sisters are the crab grass in the lawn of life.
—**Charles M. Schulz**

You can kid the world but not your sister.
—**Charlotte Gray**

I can't remember if I'm the good sister or the evil one.
—**Anonymous**

What are sisters for if not to point out the things the rest of the world is too polite to mention.
—**Claire Cook**

So Chic
THE INSPIRATION

Our aunt Margie, Patsy's twin, got married and relocated to California. Prior to the move, we were lucky to have our favorite aunt live with us until we were flower girls in her wedding at ages six and eight. In the years before her departure, we can remember many sister dinners at the kitchen table marked by squeals of laughter until the wee hours. Sometimes legions of girlfriends would be included, but mostly, it was just the two of them sharing marvelous secrets that we will never know.

The idea for this book was also fueled as a way for Babs and me to spend quality time together. Because our parents died so young, we have always hung on to each other like hands on a roller coaster . . . that tight. We realize that, sure, we could fight because of our minute differences like some sisters, but the two of us are the only Slageter family that we have, so she tolerates my incessant calls when I cook anything, and I take a deep breath when she's (always) bossy. As adults we have resided thousands of miles apart. Luckily, even when long distance-timed calls (between San Francisco and London) were exorbitantly expensive, we managed to finagle a daily chat. Our understanding husbands knew from day one that the routine call was a mandatory part of the relocation package, more economical than paying a shrink and not negotiable.

Ever since we were little, Mom would tell us, "After I am in heaven, I will be asking God to paint our favorite sunset, so when you see a beautiful pink sky, that's me reminding you to call your sister." Works every time.

My younger son would frequently come running to the back door while playing in the yard just long enough to tell me, "Look, Mimi and God are painting the sky again!" I was telling this to a friend, and he said, "That will work for me too. When I see a rainbow, I will call my brother!" Love that.

So please help Patsy earn her wings; look up at that glorious pink sky, and call your siblings.

48

- One axiom: gin and tonics, vodka tonics, and red licorice always produce a successful Sisters' Dinner.

- Growing up, we adored the colors pink and green and really never tired of that combination. So plan a dinner or lunch surrounded by all things you love and your favorite childhood colors.

- Have napkins made with your sister's or family's most used word or expression: "Stop It!" hot pink napkins were a birthday present from a friend since we say it so frequently.

- Every party has to have funny napkins. Party stores have great conversation-starter, funny paper napkins.

- Find bottles of wine with unusual names. We liked this bottle of vitamins.

- For arrangements, we love flowers that are right out of the garden, so go outside and cut flowering shrubs in your backyard like this viburnum pictured from Wayside Gardens.

- Actually, it's a great idea to plant some flowering plants such as lilacs, viburnum, gardenias, peonies, camellias, and roses. I even have a rose bush in a pot that blooms profusely. Go to the website of David Austin Roses and order some beauties online.

- Inexpensive pink and green cabbage plates can be found in department stores or on eBay.

- Even the glasses are cabbage leaves. My friend Jo started giving these many years ago. Rather than lighting another perfunctory candle on birthdays and holidays, start a glass collection. Everyone can use more of those.

Menu

ARTICHOKE SPREAD

HALIBUT WITH
LEMONS AND CAPERS

TOMATO TART WITH
MOZZARELLA AND
FRESH BASIL

SPINACH LEAF SALAD

CARMELITE BARS

ARTICHOKE SPREAD

Many artichoke dips and spreads taste and feel heavy. I came up with this lighter version, and it spreads easily even on thin crackers.

1 12-ounce jar artichokes, drained and chopped

1 small purple onion, chopped

3 radishes, chopped

4 tablespoons whipped chive cream cheese

2 tablespoons skim milk

1 cup shredded cheddar cheese

Mix all ingredients and serve with your favorite crackers. I like English-style table water crackers, as they have a nice crisp taste and snap, you know, like a nun's fingers when she wants a student's attention.

HALIBUT WITH LEMONS AND CAPERS

Some of my recipes that are not passed down generationally in our family come from ideas that we find in restaurants around the world. This wonderful halibut recipe comes from a dinner my husband had on an Alaskan fishing trip. This fish is tasty, and the capers add just that little extra tang. Try it, just for the halibut.

1½ pounds halibut or your favorite firm
    white fish, skinless

Salt

Pepper

Paprika

3 tablespoons olive oil

2 tablespoons lemon juice

¼ cup capers

Season the fish on both sides with salt, pepper, and paprika. Heat olive oil in a skillet over medium heat. Add the fish and cook for 5 minutes. Turn the fish over, adding the lemon juice and capers to the skillet. Cook 5 minutes and remove from heat.

And, for a change of pace, prepare this recipe with boneless, skinless chicken breast. Pound the chicken breast and season and cook as above.

Serves 6

SPINACH LEAF SALAD

It might seem obsessive-compulsive, but I always remove the stems from spinach and arugula leaves. Your guests will definitely appreciate it.

6-ounce bag fresh spinach

½ cup pomegranate seeds

1 small red onion, sliced

Remove the stems from the spinach leaves (as we've already discussed). Place on a platter. Sprinkle with pomegranate seeds and red onion.

DRESSING
1 teaspoon Dijon mustard

2 tablespoons white balsamic vinegar

1 teaspoon honey

½ teaspoon salt

½ teaspoon pepper

¼ cup olive oil

¼ cup Parmesan cheese, grated thickly

Mix the mustard, vinegar, honey, salt, and pepper together. Drizzle in the olive oil. Add the Parmesan cheese. Serve in an appropriate vessel to allow your guests to portion their own; that would be the one that looks elegant and is easy to use, even a ceramic gravy boat in a pinch.

Serves 6

TOMATO TART WITH MOZZARELLA AND FRESH BASIL

Pizza this is not. Served as a side with the fish or chicken, this dish is very light and tasty. Easy to make and everyone will like it. Sister Mary Redempta would approve of this on meatless Fridays.

1 Pillsbury pie crust

3 fresh tomatoes

2 cups shredded mozzarella cheese

½ cup fresh basil, sliced

Line a 12-inch tart pan with the pie crust. Poke the crust a few times with a fork. Place tomatoes on the crust; salt and pepper to taste. Top with the cheese and basil. In a preheated oven, bake at 375 degrees for 15 minutes.

Serves 6

CARMELITE BARS

Pun intended. We also served, apropos the theme, angel food cake and devil's food cake, but don't tell Sister Mary Katherine; we bought the cakes at our favorite bakery.

¾ cup dark brown sugar

¼ cup butter

1 egg

1 cup flour

¼ teaspoon salt

1 teaspoon baking powder

1 teaspoon vanilla extract

½ cup chocolate chips

½ cup butterscotch chips

Melt the brown sugar and butter together and allow to cool. Add the rest of the ingredients. Put in a pie plate sprayed with baking spray. In a pre-heated oven, bake for 20 minutes at 350 degrees.

Makes 16 bars

TABLE 4

THE SISTERS DINNER

So Slageter

Quit that rubbernecking and stop talking to your neighbor.
—**SISTER MARIE REPARATA**

Hearing nuns' confessions is like being stoned to death with popcorn.
—**BISHOP FULTON SHEEN**

The only difference between a saint and a sinner is that every saint has a past and every sinner has a future.
—**OSCAR WILDE**

Then Sister Aquinata abandoned the nonviolent methods and produced a rolling pin from somewhere.
—**MARY ROBINETTE KOWAL**

People, don't use your playground voice in the classroom.
—**SISTER JAMES IRENE**

I'm a good Catholic girl. The faith has always been elusive, but the guilt is intractable.
—**JANET EVANOVICH**

That's a detention, Miss Mutation.
—**SISTER MERECI**
in Biology class, commenting on Sue Sue's chemically streaked, blonde hair

We go to Heaven for the climate and Hell for the company.
—**MARK TWAIN**

Our parish priests' calendars were filled with nightly invitations from parishioners anxious to wine and dine them in their homes and clubs.

On the other hand, all of the Dominican Sisters who taught at our school were forbidden to accept any celebratory outside invitations. Our parents lamented their plight and decided to take action. About a week prior to major holidays and the eve of snow days, Dad would hand-deliver two cases of "grape juice" to the convent doorstep so at least they could celebrate together privately. Initially he was met at the door with trepidation and one tentative "thank you" from the door-duty nun, but as the years progressed, the nuns' exuberance and appreciation grew and so did the numbers who greeted him at the door. Babs and I overheard a few details of this escapade and devised a way to be included to help. We quickly fashioned our own nun habits and veils out of numerous bath towels, saddle shoes, and Dad's belts, with dangling rosaries. When Mom saw us, she was laughing so hard that the Slageter girls were added to the Easter delivery team. In retrospect, this is probably the reason that our math skills are OK. We had to get passing grades for fear the deliveries would stop.

Some of our favorite dedicated teachers and our aunt, Sister Mary Kathryn, initiated our early fascination and love of nuns. As you can see in this picture, our collection of nunabelia is noteworthy and started with our Madame Alexander nun dolls from Santa. We have always been inundated with nun cards, calendars, aprons, cups, ornaments, and nunzillas from our friends in the know for every occasion. We are running out of room for this collection; we really must break this habit. (Sorry.)

- Start collecting. Nun objects are available in party stores and online. These nunzillas are hung over the table with invisible fishing line.

- Pure white lilies are the flowers of choice.

- The large nuns-on-lake painting was bought at an art fair in Beaver Creek, Colorado. Hubby, just ten minutes before, had purchased an expensive painting of pink peonies for my birthday . . . but then I saw the ice-skating nuns and had to have them. He thought I was kidding. And guess who got the same painting for her birthday that year? Babs!

- The painting of two nuns beneath was painted by our talented friend Jane for a unique birthday gift. If you are artistic, paint a small canvas of one of your friend's favorite items. It will be treasured for all time.

- Our nuns' habits are from the costume store BuyCostumes.com.

- Our blow-up Bad Dolly is in detention for smoking and other demerits for who knows what. She is wearing a school uniform, also from a costume store.

- On the birthday of one of our friends who attended Sacred Heart Academy, we made the seventy-five nun veils out of poster board and black cotton from the fabric store. (Make sure there are two hairpins on each.) Everyone at the party (women AND men) wore the veils and serenaded her with the song "How do you solve a problem like Maria?" The words were personalized by another friend. Once again, parties are so much more fun when you share the preparations with a pal.

- Don't forget the party favors . . . rulers.

WE LIKE THE SONG "SISTERS":

Sisters, Sisters
There were never such devoted sisters.
Never had to have a chaperone, no sir.
I'm here to keep my eye on her.

Caring, sharing
Every little thing that we are wearing.
When a certain gentleman arrives from Rome,
She wore the dress and I stayed home.

All kinds of weather,
We stick together,
The same in the rain or sun.

Two different faces,
But in tight places
We think and act as one.

Those who've seen us
Know that not a thing could come between us.
Many men have tried to split us up,
but no one can.

Lord help the mister
Who comes between me and my sister,
And Lord help the sister
who comes between me and my man.

TABLE

5

THE LITTLE
PRINCESS
BIRTHDAY

So Chic

A girl must be two things: classy and fabulous.
—COCO CHANEL

Little girls love dolls. They don't love doll clothes. We've got four thousand dolls and ain't one of them got a stitch of clothes on.
—JEFF FOXWORTHY

If only girls came with pull-down menus and online help.
—UNKNOWN

If a girl looks swell when she meets you, who gives a damn if she's late?
—J.D. SALINGER
CATCHER IN THE RYE

They say that girls are the ones that want fairytale endings, but then again, who are the authors of fairytales? Mostly men . . .
—ALINA RADOI

Good girls go to heaven, bad girls go everywhere.
—MAE WEST

There are only three things women need in life: food, water, and compliments.
—CHRIS ROCK

All unsupervised little girls will be given chocolate and a kitty.
—UNKNOWN

Mom loved to celebrate birthdays, and for Babs's eighth-year celebration, she outdid herself, transforming our dining room into a jaw-dropping princess heaven. Oodles of kickball-sized flowers made of pastel tissue paper fluttered above the table brimming with candy and daisies. Chair backs were adorned with grosgrain polka dot ribbons and our most-coveted treat, the all-day lollipop. Little darlings dressed in their Sunday best were dropped off, ready to feast on cake and ice cream. Everyone was anxiously awaiting the Saturday afternoon festivity. One friend, Bevie, still recounts the story of her playground promise to bring a Ken doll as her present if Babs would add her to the party guest list.

The girls were ushered to their embellished seats, where they discovered that each girl's plate contained a rock candy bracelet and a pearl necklace party favor, ready to wear. The food consisted of platters of bite-size, variously shaped sandwiches made of ham and cheese, chicken salad, and egg salad. Not a rubbery piece of chicken or pea to be found. A large vase filled with jellybeans was stationed on the table, and if you guessed the number, that was your take-home prize.

As the afternoon progressed, activities moved to the family room, where the usual game involving donkeys, blindfolds, and tails transpired. Musical chairs, hula hoop, and twist contests were also completed; the winners were awarded prizes such as hair bows and new pencil cases. Next it was the compulsory circle as everyone watched the honoree open each and every present. After a riveting game of "Party Line," it was time to say (in a sing-songy voice), "Thank you, Mrs. Slageter!," hug, and go home.

But wait, now, where is the Birthday Girl? Alone in her room with the door shut playing with all of her new Madame Alexander dolls and . . . no Ken doll. Sorry, Bevie.

- We ordered most of the items for this table from Party City.

- Have to warn you: the tissue paper balls take some time to fluff, so do ahead.

- The candy was bought on an online site, but we found that the party stores have an ample supply of candy.

- Also, to make this look like more candy, we used rolled-up paper under the top layers for bulk.

- For the floral flower balls, start with oasis, bought at craft stores. These need to be soaked in a bucket of water for twenty minutes. Sheets of green moss are applied, using floral pins; be sure to leave little spaces for the flowers. Cut short stems on the carnations, Gerber daisies, and mums; just push them into the ball. We got these silver stands at the craft store, but you could put them on cake stands or right on the table.

- The circus glasses were our grandmother's, but until she passed, no one was allowed to touch. We are not sure why she cherished these, as we were not aware of any circus performers in our family.

- We did not have a tablecloth, so we took two drapery panels right off the rods and used them for the party. Just use placemats.

- The tiered, silver centerpiece is from Two's Company.

- The name tags on this table are female book characters, each girl's favorite heroine.

- Use name cards to show the food choices; glue little chicks for the chicken salad, etc.

- Our Mean Girl blow-up dolly is placed in time-out because she opened one of the birthday girl's gifts. Tsk tsk! She does look cute in her Kate Spade dress, though.

Menu

STRAWBERRY
AND CUCUMBER
OPEN-FACE SANDWICHES

HAM AND CHEESE
SANDWICHES

EGG SALAD SANDWICHES

CHICKEN SALAD

PINK LEMONADE

ICED TEA

COCONUT DOLL CAKE

Egg Salad

Chick Salad

PINK LEMONADE

Don't be silly. What other color lemonade would you have for a Princesses' Party?

½ cup sugar

½ cup water

12 lemons, juiced

4 cups water

2 tablespoons cherry juice

Mix sugar and water and simmer for 5 minutes to make a simple syrup. Add all the ingredients and stir.

Serves 4 to 6

ICED TEA

It's a little girls' party, and you can be certain that some won't like lemonade, no matter the pretty color. Make some of this classic favorite and serve it in a pretty pitcher.

8 cups boiling water

¼ cup sugar

8 tea bags

Mix water and sugar. Add tea bags and steep for 20 minutes.

Serves 4 to 6

HAM AND CHEESE SANDWICHES

This is not the corner deli version unless your local deli makes darling, flower-shaped sandwiches. You will also not find these in a lunch pail, but you will find that even the pickiest girl at the party will love this tasty treat. These are adorable and easy.

1 loaf thin white bread

Ham salad

½ pound Swiss cheese

HAM SALAD

1 cup chopped ham

2 tablespoons red pepper, chopped

1 tablespoon yellow mustard

2 tablespoons mayonnaise or plain Greek yogurt

2 tablespoons green onion, chopped

2 tablespoons Worcestershire sauce

½ teaspoon salt

½ teaspoon ground black pepper

Mix all salad ingredients and follow assembly directions below.

With a flower-shaped cookie cutter, cut the bread to make 2 sandwiches for each girl. Assemble the sandwiches, layering the ham salad and cheese.

Makes 16 sandwiches

STRAWBERRY AND CUCUMBER OPEN-FACE SANDWICHES

Girls of all ages love these pretty and delicious round-shaped sandwiches. We have served these many times at birthday parties and teas. Make some extras for the moms.

1 loaf thin white bread

1 container whipped strawberry cream cheese

2 cucumbers, sliced thin

With a round-shaped cookie cutter, cut the bread to make 2 sandwiches for each girl. Spread with cream cheese. Top with cucumber.

Makes 20 open-face sandwiches

EGG SALAD SANDWICHES

The hits from the old family recipes just keep on coming. We can't remember a Friday growing up when this wasn't lunch. Try it as a stand-alone salad served over greens or make a sandwich using good rye or whole wheat bread. It also works well on toasted thin white bread.

8 eggs

¼ cup yellow mustard

1 tablespoon light mayonnaise or plain Greek yogurt

½ teaspoon salt

½ teaspoon black pepper

2 tablespoons dill pickle, diced

3 tablespoons diced celery

Put eggs in a pot and fill with cold water to cover eggs. Bring to a boil. Boil 1 minute, then turn heat to a steady simmer for 15 minutes. Let eggs cool in water. Peel and chop eggs. Mix with the rest of the ingredients.

Makes 4 sandwiches or 12 tea sandwiches

CHICKEN SALAD

Our twist on a family favorite makes this salad come alive.

BAKED CHICKEN BREAST

Definitely use this method of cooking chicken breasts for salads (see below) or any recipe that calls for baked chicken. We think it's great served for dinner.

4 chicken breast halves with skin and bones

1 lemon, juiced

Fox Point Seasoning from Penzeys

1 cup chicken broth

Lift skin on each chicken breast; sprinkle lemon juice and the seasoning on both sides of the skin. Place in a baking dish and pour the chicken broth around the chicken. Bake at 450 degrees for 40 minutes. Remove from oven, cover with foil, and allow to cool.

CHICKEN SALAD

3 chicken breasts, cooked and shredded or cubed

4 green onions, sliced

1 cup red grapes, cut in halves

½ cup roasted pecans

¼ cup parsley, chopped

Mix all of the above ingredients.

DRESSING

½ cup light mayo or plain Greek yogurt

¼ cup hot mango chutney

1 lime, juiced

1 teaspoon salt

½ teaspoon black pepper

1 teaspoon curry powder

Mix all these ingredients and then mix with the chicken mixture.

Serves 6

COCONUT DOLL CAKE

Oh my, what little girl wouldn't love this adorable doll cake? Such great pleasure for so little work, and this is your little Princess, right? Make it a tradition of your own. (Easier than you think. It's sheet cake and cream cheese frosting.)

1 stick butter

½ cup canola oil

1½ cups sugar

5 eggs, yolks and whites separated and retained

1 cup milk

1 lemon, juiced

2 cups flour

1 teaspoon baking soda

1 teaspoon vanilla extract

2 cups shredded coconut

BATTER FOR SHEET CAKE AND DOLL CAKE

In the bowl of an electric mixer, cream the butter, oil, and sugar. Add egg yolks one at a time, beating the mixture after each addition. Separately mix the milk and lemon juice and set aside. Separately mix the flour and baking soda. With the mixer running, alternate adding the flour and milk. Now add the vanilla and coconut. Beat the egg whites until stiff and then fold into the cake batter. Spray a 9x13-inch baking pan with PAM and add the batter. Bake at 325 degrees for 45 minutes. Allow to cool. Now you have a sheet cake.

DOLL CAKE

1 2-quart Pyrex round baking dish

1 1½-quart Pyrex round baking dish

1 10-ounce Pyrex round baking dish

1 doll head and torso from a craft store

To create the doll cake, use the same ingredients and process as for the sheet cake, except for the pan. Divide the batter into baking dishes sprayed with PAM. Bake the 2 larger cakes at 325 degrees for 35 minutes. Bake the smaller cake at 325 degrees for 18 minutes. Allow cakes to cool.

FROSTING FOR SHEET CAKE / DOUBLE INGREDIENTS FOR THE DOLL CAKE

4 ounces cream cheese, room temperature

½ stick butter, room temperature

½ teaspoon vanilla extract

½ of a 1-pound box of powdered sugar

Mix all ingredients. Frost the sheet cake.

DOLL CAKE ASSEMBLY

In descending size (largest on the bottom), layer the cooled cakes with frosting between each layer. The two larger-sized form the skirt, and the smaller size the torso. Put the doll figurine into the top and ice everything. Smiling yet?

TABLE
5

THE BAMM-BAMM BIRTHDAY PARTY

So Slageter

The sole purpose of a child's middle name is so he can tell when he's really in trouble.

—**Unknown**

My three brothers and I knew how to fix house damage at eight years old. We would dry wall, spackle, and paint before Dad got home.

—**Ryan Reynolds**

We live in a society where pizza gets to your house before the police.

—**Unknown**

George Washington, as a boy, was ignorant of the commonest accomplishment of youth. He could not even lie.

—**Mark Twain**

Of all the animals, the boy is the most unmanageable.

—**Plato**

Boys are beyond the range of anybody's sure understanding, at least when they are between the ages of eighteen months and ninety years.

—**James Thurber**

Why do boys believe you when you say there are four billion stars but check when you say the paint is wet?

—**Unknown**

A mother takes twenty years to make a man out of her boy, and another woman can make a fool of him in twenty minutes.

—**Robert Frost**

So Slageter
THE INSPIRATION

Babs has girls; Sue Sue has boys.

During the extra active crabby chair (time-out) years, our combined family vacations were strained, then dwindled. Granted, I will admit that our family branch did require visits to emergency rooms from Martha's Vineyard to Orlando.

In our house, no one ever sat still, and everything was copacetic unless we saw blood. Meanwhile, at Babs's house, the girls colored and painted meticulously for hours. You only knew if they were alive by the glimpse of an infrequent, bobbing hair bow.

Coming from an all-girl, princess-party background, I had no idea how to entertain a group of rambunctious boys. On a seventh birthday, we hosted a darling train-themed event that was an absolute disaster. The conductor hats became Frisbees, and the homemade caboose cake, minus five licorice wheels, had obviously been taste-tested before the birthday song. Just thinking about the sound of twenty-five authentic locomotive wooden whistles can bring on a major headache and twitches. Oh wait; then there was the cleanup.

Because of that fiasco and to avoid my feeling that we were entertaining the wannabe cast from *Lord of the Flies*, the ninth birthday celebration and every one thereafter followed this list:

1. Remove anything that is remotely valuable from the backyard, including most furniture, chair cushions, plants, and growing basil, and secure un-cemented brick walkways (not kidding).
2. Scatter twenty-five balls for every sport except bowling and handball.
3. Hire high school boys to explain the activities, play the "Wrap the Mummy" game, and later, distribute the silly string.
4. Call pizza delivery. Order double the amount you had planned to order. Tip the delivery man well so that he will return next year. You will not need plates or cutlery, as all pizza will disappear before boxes are placed on table.
5. Just in case pizza man is detained, heat up five hundred pigs-in-a-blanket (always in freezer).
6. For the refreshments, make sure the hose is connected. Do not forget to remove the spray nozzle.
7. Lock every house entrance door.
8. Optimistically, put a roll of paper towels and a box of Kleenex outside the locked door.
9. Watch like an eagle from behind the curtain, armed with a whistle, the phone pre-programmed to 911, and an adult beverage.
10. Clean up the backyard for five hours. Pray for rain.
11. Return the random kid back to his nanny after you find his clothes and his other shoe.
12. Take an Advil and thank God that you have 364 days till the next birthday.
13. Laugh every day. Read the comic strip *Zits* in your local paper. You can also type "zits comics images" on your smartphone or get the book *A Zits Guide to Living with Your Teenager*. This is imperative. You will come to realize that all of the above is normal boy behavior. You are not alone. The wisdom gleaned from this comic strip has diffused many father/son confrontations, and other moms of boys (hi to Allison and Kathy) frequently say thanks for sharing this gem.

So Slageter
THE SISTERS' SCOOP

- What's that stringy white stuff? Silly string, of course. Buy it wholesale by the case at Zurchers. Boys love this activity, but this does entail at least a five-hour cleanup. This should be a once-in-a-lifetime event. Just in case you need some help, who ya gonna call? The Maids of Dupage County (a service available in several locations throughout the country).

- Divide into two-man teams. Give each team one roll of bathroom tissue. One boy wraps the other from head to toe. First team to use all the paper is the winner. Then reverse for second game. The prize is verbal: "You are the winner."

- Suggest a bathroom break before the game starts. As you can see, our mummy friend in the picture wasn't offered that option.

- Don't kid yourself; all boys drink right out of the family dairy carton. So if you want to get fancy, offer them their own pint of milk.

- Notice we did play one game of "Wrap the Mummy."

- "Wrap the Mummy" game, part two:

- Give a large garbage bag to each team. Explain that the team whose bag is the fullest and placed on the driveway when the timer rings (seven minutes) gets the prize. Award two whoopee cushions from Stupid.com. There still will be the five-hour cleanup.

- Candy sticks were a big hit at our school carnival, made with hardware-store short wooden dowels, bulk candy, and glue guns. We also covered heavy plastic pitchforks from Party City with candy. If you do succumb to this idea, only give these party favors on the way out of your house. Think about it.

- Forget about this Sisters' Scoop section and hold firm to above simple checklist.

TABLE
6

DAD'S HAPPY FIFTIETH

So Chic

You don't stop laughing because you've grown old. You grow old because you stop laughing.
—**ANONYMOUS**

The man who views the world at fifty the same as he did at twenty has wasted thirty years of his life.
—**MUHAMMAD ALI**

Looking fifty is great . . . if you are sixty.
—**JOAN RIVERS**

Birthdays are nature's way of telling us to eat more cake.
—**ANONYMOUS**

I'm at an age where my back goes out more than I do.
—**PHYLLIS DILLER**

Do not worry about avoiding temptation; as you grow older, it will avoid you.
—**JOEY ADAMS**

Youth is when you are allowed to stay up late on New Year's Eve; middle age is when you are forced to.
—**BILL VAUGHAN**

Laughter is not at all a bad beginning for a friendship, and it is by far the best ending for one.
—**OSCAR WILDE**

As we were growing up, Dad convinced the family that we were given a school holiday solely because it was his birthday. It was years before we figured out that December 8 was a Catholic holy day for all parochial and private school children. The day began with 7:30 mass, where every morning Artsie was an usher. He was extremely devout, but during the fifteen minutes of collection duty, he upheld his reputation as the entertaining usher. If he knew you, which was likely, you could be a target. He was most famous for the lingering-basket maneuver, which entailed mercilessly shaking that long pole until more money was deposited. Even from our vantage point in the last pew, we were always cognizant of his shenanigans by just watching the parishioners' shoulders vibrating with laughter as he progressed.

On the ride home from church, just as we were whining in the back seat about our upheaval from a cozy flannel bed on our free day, his imposing Chrysler New Yorker would miraculously land smack-dab in front of Conrad's Bakery. Oh, the appeasing power of hot chocolate and fresh-from-the-oven glazed donuts with sprinkles.

For Dad's birthday dinner, one thing was a given: meatloaf was his requested menu. As much as he loved it, Patsy hated it. Apparently our parents had been invited to someone's home and our mother was appalled "that anyone would have the gall to serve meatloaf at a Saturday night dinner party!" Because of this, Dad's birthday was the only meatloaf night of the year, and the invited guests were men only. However, as Mom perfected the recipe and concocted a tasty topping, this eventually became the family's and friends' favorite; in later years, we were all included in the annual meatloaf celebration. However, Patsy held her ground and believed that we all only craved it because we had to wait a whole year. We do know that there was no meatloaf dinner when December 8 fell on a Saturday.

- These candelabra usually reside on the mantel but look regal, so we used them as a centerpiece. Find objects around your house or thrift store and rethink their purpose; use them in an unexpected way.

- These chargers have the look of silver but are plastic (about $1.99 each at Hobby Lobby).

- The large, domed silver piece on table center could be intimidating; to negate the formality, we filled it with Dad's favorite candy—red licorice. Use serious wedding gifts or auction finds in a new, informal way.

- We love carnations. They are inexpensive and can be massed pavé-style in any bowl or vase or in cups at every setting.

- Make sure to fill the table with the birthday honoree's favorites. You'll notice the bourbon, red licorice, peanuts, a glass candy jar resembling his beloved Boston terrier, and "vegetables that taste like candy" (Artsie's favorite ploy).

- Can't have too many dessert plates in our book; these checkered black-and-white plates are from Target.

Menu

PUFF PASTRY ROUNDS

APPETIZER SAUSAGE

MOM'S MEATLOAF

DOUBLE-BAKED POTATOES

CANDIED VEGGIES

PATSY'S APPLE PIE

RASPBERRY-BLUEBERRY
CRUMBLE

So Chic
RECIPES

PUFF PASTRY ROUNDS

Here is a recipe that we frequently serve with an Italian dinner or any time as an hors d'oeuvre with wine and cocktails. Always keep some puff pastry dough in the freezer. It works well with many toppings.

1 red pepper, diced

1 onion, diced

1 to 2 tablespoons olive oil

1 cup goat cheese

2 tablespoons Parmesan cheese

½ cup chopped pepperoni

Puff pastry sheets

1 egg, beaten with 1 tablespoon water

2 tablespoons basil

Sauté pepper and onion in 1 to 2 tablespoons olive oil. Mix with cheeses and pepperoni. Cut pastry sheet into small rounds or squares. Place on cookie sheets. Brush with egg mixture. Top pastry rounds with cheese mixture. Preheat oven to 375 degrees; bake for 10 minutes. Garnish with basil. (May be assembled hours ahead. Bake when ready to serve.)

Makes 2 dozen rounds

APPETIZER SAUSAGE

I have found this to be a favorite appetizer for all the men in my life. I'm sure your guys will love it as well.

6 brats

Pot of whole grain mustard

Toothpicks for serving

Grill or broil the brats and slice to mouth-size serving portions. We'll leave that sizing to you. Serve with whole grain mustard for dipping, using the toothpicks. Discourage fingers; that's like double-dipping.

MOM'S MEATLOAF

I am not kidding; every one of the guys related to a Slageter sister will do cartwheels for Patsy's meatloaf.

2 tablespoons olive oil

1 small onion, chopped

2 ribs of celery, chopped

2 cloves of garlic, chopped

1 teaspoon salt

½ teaspoon cayenne pepper

½ teaspoon red Tabasco sauce

1 tablespoon Worcestershire sauce

½ cup milk

½ cup ketchup

2 pounds ground beef

2 eggs, beaten

1 cup Italian-style bread crumbs

Heat olive oil in a medium saucepan. Sauté the onion, celery, and garlic until soft. Add salt, cayenne, Tabasco, Worcestershire, milk, and ketchup. Set aside. In a large bowl, mix the beef, eggs, and bread crumbs. Mix in the veggie mixture. Form into a loaf. Place in a 9x13-inch baking dish. Pour ¾ cup water around the loaf.

MEATLOAF TOPPING

¾ cup ketchup

2 tablespoons dark brown sugar

1 teaspoon dry mustard

Mix ingredients and spread on top of the meatloaf.

Bake at 350 degrees for 1 hour.

Serves 6 to 8

DOUBLE-BAKED POTATOES

3 large baking potatoes

3 tablespoons whipped cream cheese

¼ to ½ cup skim milk

½ cup cottage cheese

Salt to taste

1½ cups shredded cheddar cheese

3 green onions, chopped

Preheat oven to 400 degrees. Bake potatoes for 1 hour or until tender. Remove and cut in half lengthwise. Scoop out the potato pulp and reserve the skins. Mash the potatoes with cream cheese and milk until smooth. Add cottage cheese, salt, cheddar cheese, and green onions. Stuff the mixture into the reserved potato skins. Bake at 350 degrees for 20 minutes.

Serves 6

RASPBERRY-BLUEBERRY CRUMBLE

Why not? The guys will love the choice of dessert.

2 pints raspberries

1 pint blueberries

¼ cup dark brown sugar

2 tablespoons flour

1 teaspoon cinnamon

Mix in a medium bowl. Place in a 7-inch baking pan sprayed with PAM.

TOPPING

¼ cup flour

¼ cup sugar

¼ cup dark brown sugar

3 tablespoons butter

½ teaspoon cinnamon

¼ cup oatmeal

Mix and crumble evenly on top of fruit. Bake at 375 degrees for 25 minutes.

CANDIED VEGGIES

Artsie often took us to lunch in downtown Cincinnati. He loved a restaurant named the Colonnade. It is here that he coined the phrase "The veggies are so good they taste just like candy!" Here is our version.

2 tablespoons olive oil

6 carrots, peeled and sliced thin

6-ounce package fresh French-cut green beans

1 red onion, chopped

1½ teaspoons salt

3 teaspoons sugar

In a large skillet, heat the oil over medium heat. Add veggies and cook for 10 minutes, stirring occasionally. Sprinkle the veggies with salt and sugar.

Serves 6

PATSY'S APPLE PIE

Our favorite, from Mom with love.

1 unbaked pie shell

FILLING

6 green apples, peeled and sliced

¼ cup sugar

¼ cup brown sugar, light or dark

2 tablespoons flour

1½ teaspoons cinnamon

Mix all in a medium-size bowl and set aside.

TOPPING

¼ cup butter, softened

½ cup flour

¼ cup sugar

¼ cup brown sugar

1 teaspoon cinnamon

Mix all.

Place apples in pie shell. Sprinkle topping over the apples. Bake at 400 degrees for 35 minutes.

TABLE
6

DAD'S SWINGING HALF-CENTURY, NO-WOMEN-ALLOWED CLUB

So Slageter

May the hinges of our friendship never grow rusty.
—**IRISH PROVERB**

None are so old as those who have outlived enthusiasm.
—**HENRY DAVID THOREAU**

Love is blind. Friendship closes its eyes.
—**FRIEDRICH NIETZSCHE**

You are only young once, but you can be immature for a lifetime.
—**JOHN P. GRIER**

Fifty is a weird age. I can clearly remember my childhood, but I can't remember where I put my keys.
—**MELANIE WHITE**

All of life is peaks and valleys. Don't let the peaks get too high and the valleys too low.
—**COACH JOHN WOODEN**

Turning fifty means it's only a matter of time before you are regaling your grandkids with details of your first colonoscopy.
—**GREG TAMBLYN**

I refuse to admit I'm fifty-two even if that does make my sons illegitimate.
—**NANCY ASTOR**

So Slageter
THE INSPIRATION

The things that we loved about our parents' friends were that they were mischievous, over-the-top funny, and extremely adept at creating fun, especially the men. As the title connotes, on their fiftieth birthdays, they were inducted into the august Swinging Half-Century Club with great fanfare, ultimately earning a knighthood. The unsuspecting birthday boy would be invited to a poker night, sporting event, or breakfast cookout as a ruse, and then the grand knights (already age fifty) held court. The elaborate setting was hysterical, with the gaudy, cartoonish throne dictating the decorum. Crowns, homemade plumed helmets, and lettered sweatshirts added the authenticity, and bourbon added the merriment. To them, reaching this lucky age surrounded by cronies had true meaning, an accomplishment begging to be celebrated. Instead of dreading and hushing this milestone, they eagerly counted down the days. In contrast, we observed that the sense of exultation of finally reaching this milestone was not a feeling shared by any of their spouses.

- We found huge gold plaster crowns on sale at Michaels, but you can use your favorite craft store.

- Giant butcher knives at each place helped display the knightly look.

- Use wire to hang plastic swords in the chandelier.

- We replaced the candelabra with outside lanterns from Costco and Pottery Barn. Be sure to affix felt on bottom to protect table.

- The plastic chalices were bought online at Oriental Trading.

- We ordered the lettered T-shirts from CustomTshirts.

- Dad's club members actually wore their shirts to every induction.

- The crown is available, thanks to a prom king in the family. ("Mooooom! Stop it!")

- The helmets were made from one sheet each of silver poster paper and large feathers, available at hobby stores.

- Dad's group had an ornate wooden throne. We frequently see gaudy oversize chairs at consignment stores that would work perfectly. For our reenactment party, we had an artist friend (thanks, Jane Corbellini) draw a simple one, easy to copy. This is made out of poster board and conveniently fits in the back of an armless chair.

- The king's robe is made out of felt from any fabric store. Gold roping and jewels are applied with a glue gun.

- The mustaches are from another favorite site, Stupid.com.

- Our blow-up doll (as King Arthur) is one of our favorite party musts. We really want to make these plastic friends respectable.

Mardi Gras Feast

Planters Punch

Mini Crab Cakes with Remoulade Sauce

Jambalaya

Cajun Sea Bass on Mashed Potatoes

Praline Parfait

Bread Pudding with Whiskey Sauce

TABLE
7

MARDI GRAS MADNESS

So Chic

Wine is constant proof that God loves us and loves to see us happy.
—**BENJAMIN FRANKLIN**

You must be excited for the one day of the year that your behavior makes sense.
—**UNKNOWN**

If you are going to do something tonight that you'll be sorry for tomorrow morning, sleep late.
—**HENNY YOUNGMAN**

When I read about the evils of drinking, I gave up reading.
—**UNKNOWN**

Remember the seven deadly sins, and have a great week.
—**UNKNOWN**

Alcohol: because no great story ever began with a salad.
—**UNKNOWN**

New Orleans is like that bad-kid island in *Pinocchio*.
—**JONAH HILL**

You should celebrate the end of a love affair as they celebrate death in New Orleans, with songs, laughter, dancing, and a lot of wine.
—**FRANÇOISE SAGAN**

The whole family loved to visit during the seven years that we lived in New Orleans. We all enjoyed sipping fiery Bloody Marys in charming, hidden courtyards while planning our next incredible meal. On numerous occasions, we were spellbound by impromptu jazz parades and would be induced by a twenty-six-ounce Pat O'Brien's hurricane to march right along.

People-watching was Dad's forte and number-one activity anywhere. He frequently advised us, "You will never be bored if you just watch the peeps!" So, with this in mind, you can imagine how captivated he was with the unhinged, eccentric peeps in the French Quarter. The peculiar Duck Lady, who patrolled Royal Street while walking her pet duck on a rhinestone leash and wearing a gold lamé ensemble, was his favorite. A particularly chatty Lucky Dog cart vendor came in a close second.

Because of this, we never encouraged our parents to visit during Carnival. Just the notion of Artsie's head ping-ponging as he watched this kaleidoscope of characters was concerning. Not to mention the humiliating task of having to explain typical Mardi Gras events to Patsy. "Yes, Mom, that is a man wearing only pantyhose, a boa, and high heels," and, "No, you cannot tell him that he has that run in his stockings!"

On the other hand, we never missed a parade or party while we lived there. Then in later years, as we were transplanted throughout the country, we carried the spirit and energy of the Crescent City with us by having an elaborate Mardi Gras celebration at our home every year. It's truly a perfect time for a party. An ample amount of time has passed after the holidays, so everyone is primed to get out of the house, especially when they realize that Lent is imminent. To make people less intimidated, we always stipulated costume optional or to just wear panty hose, a boa, and high heels. Oh, and for the women, they could just wear anything festive or glittered.

- Each year there is a plethora of Mardi Gras decorations available at any party store, or you can go online to the Oriental Trading and Mardi Gras Outlet sites. Signature beads, doubloons, and masks are so inexpensive. You can scatter these on tables or use them in bowls, compotes, and bounteous adornment.

- Fat Tuesday colors are gold, green, and purple. Use gold items from holiday decorations too. Here, we used gold tassels as napkin rings.

- King cakes are the tradition during the season. These are cinnamon coffee cakes with icing and topped with colored sugar in Mardi Gras colors. In one piece, there is a plastic baby trinket, and if you get that slice, it's your turn to bring the cake the following week of Carnival. Order yours where the natives go: Joe Gambino's Bakery or Haydel's Bakery.

- The gold, ruffled placemats are inexpensive, from Pier 1 Imports.

- Bring out anything royal, as there actually are kings and queens of Mardi Gras.

- We used purple and lavender parrot tulips (our favorite, with ruffled edges). These are, as always, from the grocery store.

- Chocolate mask lollipops in the praline parfaits are from a local candy shop.

- One year, bolts of green, gold, and purple lamé were bought at a discount fabric store. This was great for swagging the banister in the front hall. You can also just tie a large knot in fabric about every four to five feet and then swag. Only use this for a Carnival party.

- Hang sundry beautiful masks, ribbons, and beads from the chandelier.

- Remember, Lent starts tomorrow. So it's a good idea to put out platters and buckets heaped with the things, such as chocolate, soft drinks, and desserts, that people might be excluding for six weeks. Put signs in these containers that say "Last Chance" or "Lent's Tomorrow!"

- Order cellophane bags and ribbon so guests can ride home with these temptations.

- Don't forget some good jazz playing such tunes as the "St. James Infirmary," "Basin Street Blues," and the Meters singing "They All Ask'd For You."

- After dinner, crank up "When the Saints Come Marching In." Initiate a conga line parade inside, outside, and all around your house. It's awkward at first, but bribe your most outgoing friends to start with you and the others will come around.

Menu

PLANTER'S PUNCH

CRAB CAKES

JAMBALAYA

CAJUN HALIBUT

PRALINE PARFAIT

BREAD PUDDING

MARDI GRAS COOKIES

PLANTER'S PUNCH

Enough of this happy concoction and they'll be planting you.

1 jigger dark rum

1 jigger light rum

1 jigger orange juice

2 jiggers pineapple juice

1 jigger water

1 tablespoon maraschino cherry juice

Ice

Mix and pour over the ice.

Serves 1

PRALINE PARFAIT

PRALINE SAUCE

⅓ cup water

⅓ cup dark brown sugar

¾ cup white corn syrup

1 cup chopped pecans

Boil water. Add sugar and corn syrup. Cook over low heat until mixture boils. Add pecans. Cool. Store in the fridge for up to two weeks.

PARFAIT

Vanilla ice cream

Whipping cream, whipped

Blueberries or maraschino cherries for topping

We use 6 large wine glasses. Put 1 tablespoon of the praline sauce in the bottom of each glass. Add a large cup of ice cream and pour more sauce over top. Finish with whipped cream and your choice of fruit on the top.

Serves 6

CRAB CAKES

These sidewalkers will dance enjoyably across your palate.

1 pound crabmeat

¾ cup Italian-style bread crumbs

½ cup chopped chives

Grated rind of one lemon

2 eggs, beaten

¼ cup skim milk

2 tablespoons Worcestershire sauce

2 tablespoons Dijon mustard

1 teaspoon Tabasco sauce

3 tablespoons canola oil

Mix all together; form into 24 cakes for appetizers or 6 large cakes for main course. You can use extra bread crumbs to hold the cakes together. Heat canola oil to medium-high heat; brown on each side. At this point you can freeze the crab cakes. To serve, thaw and bake in a preheated 325-degree oven for 8 minutes.

REMOULADE SAUCE

1 cup light mayonnaise

2 tablespoons Dijon mustard

2 tablespoons horseradish

½ lemon, juiced

2 tablespoons ketchup

2 tablespoons Worcestershire sauce

1 teaspoon Tabasco sauce

½ cup chopped parsley

½ cup chopped green onion

Mix all and serve with crab cakes.

Serves 6

JAMBALAYA

Well, if this is a mishmash of Cajun goodies, then let's all jump in. No need to spell or pronounce it correctly. Just enjoy.

¼ teaspoon cayenne pepper

½ teaspoon salt

½ teaspoon thyme

¼ teaspoon sage

3 boneless chicken breasts, cubed

3 tablespoons olive oil

1 small onion, chopped

1 red pepper, chopped

2 ribs celery, chopped

1 pound beef kielbasa, cubed

1 16-ounce can tomato sauce

1 28-ounce can chopped tomatoes, drained

4 cups chicken broth

2 teaspoons Cajun seasoning

1½ cups raw rice

Mix cayenne pepper, salt, thyme, and sage; sprinkle on chicken. Heat oil in a soup pot and brown the chicken. Add the rest of the ingredients. Bring to a boil, lower heat to low, and cook 1 hour or until rice is done.

Serves 6

CAJUN HALIBUT

1½ pounds halibut or other firm white fish

2 tablespoons Cajun seasoning

2 tablespoons olive oil

½ lemon, juiced

Coat fish with seasoning. Heat oil on high heat in a heavy skillet. Add fish; cook 4 minutes. Turn fish and cook 3 minutes. Add lemon juice and serve on mashed potatoes.

Serves 6

BREAD PUDDING

A wonderfully deceptive way to consume New Orleans spirits. Yes, of course: whiskey sauce.

2 cups whole milk

4 tablespoons butter

⅓ cup sugar

4 cups cubed French bread

2 eggs, beaten

1 teaspoon vanilla extract

Heat milk. Add butter and sugar. Heat until butter is melted. Pour over bread. Mix eggs and vanilla extract. Pour over ensemble. Bake in a well-greased 1½-quart dish at 350 degrees for 35 minutes.

WHISKEY SAUCE

1 cup heavy cream

½ cup sugar

1 tablespoon butter

1 teaspoon cornstarch

2 tablespoons water

2 tablespoons bourbon

Cinnamon

Heat the cream, sugar, and butter. Separately mix cornstarch and water. Add that to cream mixture. Cook until thickened. Add bourbon. This is not a thick sauce. Pour over each serving of bread pudding. Sprinkle with cinnamon.

Serves 6

MARDI GRAS COOKIES

Follow Our Grandmother's Cut-Out Sugar Cookies recipe in Table 9. For purple glaze use 2 drops blue and 4 drops red food coloring and 6 drops green food coloring for green glaze. Sprinkle with colored sugar.

TABLE
7

OH NO!
ASH WEDNESDAY
IS PAYBACK

So Slageter

Those have a short Lent, who owe money to be paid at Easter.
—**BENJAMIN FRANKLIN**

What happens in Vegas may stay in Vegas, but what happens in New Orleans goes home with you.
—**LAURELL K. HAMILTON**

Sign of a good night— you wake up with sunglasses on.
—**ANONYMOUS (HA!)**

Hangover? "Drink wine." Headache? "Drink wine." Allergies? "Drink wine." Dry eye? "Drink wine." Stubbed toe? "Drink wine." Hemorrhoids? "Drink wine."
—**MUFFIN LEMAK**

We never repent of having eaten too little.
—**THOMAS JEFFERSON**

Dear Alcohol, we had a deal where you would make me funnier, smarter, and a better dancer. I saw the video . . . we need to talk.
—**UNKNOWN**

Yes Madam, I am a drunk. But in the morning I will be sober and you will still be ugly.
—**WINSTON CHURCHILL**

I don't have a drinking problem because I had no problem drinking that bottle of wine.
—**MEEGAN GRAHAM,** FRIEND

So Slageter
THE INSPIRATION

Did you ever see those old cowboy movies where the cowpoke gallops on his horse into a desolate, abandoned mining town? Well, to me that's the appearance and feeling of New Orleans on the day after Mardi Gras. The streets are eerily empty, and the quiet is deafening. After three weeks of non-stop costume making, parties, parades, bead catching, hurricane drinking, and eating umpteen king cakes to find that implanted little plastic doll, everyone is depleted. But wait, the day after Mardi Gras is Ash Wednesday, and it's required to attend church to receive ashes. Where oh where is the Advil, and how in the world do I get up to find it? And, oh #@%*; where's our baby?!

- We begged for Dolly's dress from a best-dressed friend. Once again, you never know what is hidden in a friend's closet. Sing along now: "When we get behind closed doors . . ."

- Strong coffee is an imperative. If you want a real New Orleans experience, order café au lait and beignets from Cafe Du Monde in the French Quarter.

- First of all, rearrange (actually, mess up) the Mardi Gras table to become the hangover table that it is. This should be predictable: Alka-Seltzer, NoDoz, aspirin, Band-Aids, Bengay, vitamins C and B bottles, beads everywhere, and random balloons and socks hanging from the chandelier.

- Our guest, crossdresser Dolly, likes to show off her ink. We prefer tattoo sleeves, which are not painful or permanent. These are best worn with a watch to hide the seam. Go ahead; shock your kids, your mother-in-law, and yourself. We get ours at the online stores Stupid, Archie McPhee, and Tinsley Transfers.

- Get some ashes for your forehead or . . . Hell, just get yourself to mass.

- To simulate a famous New Orleans hurricane drink, just buy the largest glass vase at Target and add six straws. You might have to connect two or three to make them long enough. Sllluuurrrpppppp!

TABLE
8

STITCH
&BITCH

So Chic

If I stitch fast enough, does it count as an aerobic exercise?
—**UNKNOWN**

Needlepoint belts are the charm bracelets for men!
—**JIM LEE,
OUR WITTY FRIEND,
TALKING UP OUR BELTS AT
A CHARITY AUCTION**

I finally got the Slageter Lasso!
—**BRENDAN KWIATKOWSKI,
FRIEND**

Where did you get that belt?
—**EVERYONE,
TO THE MALES AND DOGS
WEARING OUR PERSONALIZED,
HANDMADE BELTS AND
COLLARS**

My own business always bores me to death. I prefer other people's.
—**OSCAR WILDE**

Introduced by Susan and Babs, I'm yet another victim to the enjoyment of the craft of needlepoint.
—**RICHARD DAVIS,
OUR PROTÉGÉ
TURNED EXPERT**

Sorry, Becky, you better not take Babs's scissors or she'll talk about you behind your back again.
—**MARY GOJKOVICH,
FRIEND**

Don't forget: you can use that lighted magnifying mirror to check for facial hair, Susan.
—**MARY MONTGOMERY,
FRIEND**

B abs had a flourishing needlepoint business in New Canaan for several years, and we have both been needlepointing since high school. Our first projects were fabulous monogrammed squares that were affixed to basket-like purses that were in vogue at the time. We then graduated to Dad's golf club covers, belts, and Christmas stockings and ornaments. A handmade needlepoint project is the perfect gift for that good friend who has everything because it's something that you can't just buy—a labor of love. I have given my design partner a Christmas ornament for the last eighteen years because I know that she cherishes every stitch and she could never sit still long enough to complete one. Monogrammed jewelry cases for travel are another item that we like to make for a good friend's special birthday. Frequent hostesses enjoy door signs that announce "Please Come In," nestled in a smart chinoiserie or bamboo border. Our spouses and college boys all proudly wear our belts and are frequently stopped by strangers inquiring how to obtain one. Of course, we are not admitting that the compliments probably have something to do with the belt images of beer labels, sport insignias, initials, alma maters, and cigars labels.

For the last three years, we have made personalized belts as auction items. Luckily, there are always competing bidders (thanks to alcohol), and these fetch thousands of dollars (more alcohol) for our favorite charities. One high bidder referred to our needlepoint belts as "charm bracelets for men." Last year's creative winning bidder requested a bucket list belt complete with a bungee jumper and Machu Picchu.

Through the years, we have both taught our hobby to many people. We thought that this would be the perfect venue to teach readers how to needlepoint in case, like us, you get antsy just sitting watching fall football or the History channel with your other half. We think that you will find this activity easy, relaxing, and more productive than four hours of Words with Friends. Oh, and if you are having any trouble learning, just call Babs anytime day or night. She will be delighted to guide you.

- Go to the websites of Rebecca Wood Designs or M's Canvashouse for beautiful canvases and yarn.

- Make sure you learn the basket-weave stitch, which moves diagonally. It offers good coverage and has even tension; furthermore, you don't have to keep turning the canvas upside down as with the continental stitch. It takes some practice to get the hang of it, but when you do, you'll never do another stitch, promise.

- For lunch, the best choice is soup and salad. You could also make dishes that can be served at room temperature. Finger foods and mini desserts are great too, always a favorite of women and easy to munch and work.

- Always remember, no matter which stitch you are using, you will be covering each plus sign (+) (coming up from the back) from bottom left to top right. With that in mind, you can't go wrong.

- Google a local needlepoint store; many offer classes. In Dallas, we go to Needlepoint This and Creative Stitches. Babs frequents House of Needlepoint in Darien, CT.

- There are also numerous sites such as YouTube, Needlepoint For Fun, and the needlepoint section at About.com that will teach you online. Watch the video guide for the basket-weave stitch.

Menu

SPINACH ENDIVE SALAD

SHRIMP ON LINGUINI

MINI CUPCAKES

SPINACH ENDIVE SALAD

This refreshing salad can also be served as an appetizer without the spinach. Just fan out the endives on a nice tray and serve. Even Rosey Grier would like this while needlepointing.

SALAD

1 6-ounce bag of fresh spinach

2 endives, separated into leaves

2 peaches, sliced thin

Goat cheese, crumbled

Toasted pecans (see below)

DRESSING

3 tablespoons white balsamic vinegar

1 teaspoon Dijon mustard

2½ teaspoons honey

½ teaspoon salt

⅓ cup canola oil

Mix vinegar, mustard, honey, and salt. Drizzle oil and mix.

TOASTED PECANS

(always have these in the fridge)

4 ounces chopped pecans

4 teaspoons melted butter

½ teaspoon salt

½ teaspoon sugar

Mix together. On a cookie sheet, bake at 350 degrees for 12 minutes or until light brown.

SERVING

Spread spinach on a serving plate. (I spoil my guests and pull off the stems.) Lay endive leaves over spinach. Put a slice of peach on each endive leaf. Sprinkle the cheese and nuts over the entire salad. Drizzle with dressing.

SHRIMP ON LINGUINI

Deliciously distracting from any needlepoint Christmas stocking or belt . . . take a little break. The shrimp sits up nicely on top of the pasta for a perfect presentation and then mixes in easy bite-size pieces. Scrumptious. We serve lunch first and then hit the canvases.

RELISH
(can be made ahead of time and refrigerated)

1 pint cherry tomatoes, cut in half

1 8-ounce jar pitted Kalamata olives, cut in half

1 small red onion, chopped

2 tablespoons olive oil

1 tablespoon fresh lemon juice

1 teaspoon honey

Mix the tomatoes, olives, and onion in a bowl. Separately whisk oil, lemon, and honey and pour over the tomato mixture. Set aside.

SHRIMP

1½ pounds medium raw shrimp, peeled and deveined

Fox Point Seasoning (Penzeys)

2 tablespoons olive oil

Season shrimp with Fox Point Seasoning. Heat oil in a large skillet over medium heat. Add shrimp and cook 1 minute on each side. Using tongs will make turning the shrimp very easy. Set aside.

LINGUINI

¼ cup olive oil

1 head of garlic, peeled and sliced (about 10 cloves)

½ teaspoon red pepper flakes

½ pound linguini, cooked and drained

In a medium saucepan, heat the olive oil, garlic, and red pepper flakes. Cook on medium heat until the garlic is light brown. Put linguine in a bowl and toss with the oil, garlic, and red pepper mixture.

PRESENTATION AND SERVING

Spread the linguini on a serving platter. Top with the tomato mixture and then with the shrimp. You can optionally garnish with sliced fresh basil and crumbled feta cheese. This is great served at room temperature.

Serves 6

MINI CUPCAKES

Serve all three types—coconut lemon, chocolate, and strawberry—and watch them fly off the tray. These are just the right size so you can taste all three.

STRAWBERRY MINI CUPCAKES

1 stick butter, softened

¾ cup sugar

½ cup frozen strawberries, diced and drained, with juice set aside

2 eggs

1¼ cups flour

1 teaspoon baking powder

¼ teaspoon salt

½ cup milk

Cream the butter and sugar until fluffy. Add the strawberries. Beat in eggs. Separately mix the flour, baking powder, and salt. Alternate adding the flour and milk to the entire mixture. Put the mixture in mini-cupcake holders. Bake at 350 degrees for 12 minutes. Let cool.

ICING
2 tablespoons butter, softened

2 tablespoons whipped cream cheese

1½ cups powdered sugar

4 to 6 tablespoons strawberry juice from frozen strawberries

Mix the whipped cream cheese, softened butter, powdered sugar, and strawberry juice thoroughly. Ice the cupcakes and cover with pearl nonpareils.

Makes 3 dozen mini cupcakes

LEMON COCONUT MINI CUPCAKES

1 stick butter, softened

¾ cup sugar

¼ cup lemon curd

2 tablespoons grated lemon rind

½ tablespoon lemon juice or ½ lemon

1 teaspoon coconut extract

2 eggs

1¼ cups flour

1 teaspoon baking powder

¼ teaspoon salt

½ cup milk

Cream the butter and sugar until fluffy. Add lemon curd, lemon rind, lemon juice, and coconut extract. Beat in eggs. Combine flour, baking powder, and salt. Add the milk to the above mixture. Put the mixture in mini-cupcake holders. Bake at 350 degrees for 12 minutes. Let cool.

ICING
2 tablespoons whipped cream cheese

2 tablespoons butter, softened

1½ cups powdered sugar

2 tablespoons lemon juice

1 cup shredded toasted coconut

Mix the whipped cream cheese, softened butter, powdered sugar, and lemon juice thoroughly. To toast the shredded coconut, spread it evenly on a cookie sheet and bake at 300 degrees for 10 minutes, stirring every 2 minutes. Use oven mitts. Ice the cupcakes and top with toasted coconut.

Makes approximately 24 mini cupcakes

CHOCOLATE MINI CUPCAKES

1 cup flour

½ cup unsweetened cocoa

½ teaspoon baking powder

½ teaspoon baking soda

½ teaspoon salt

½ cup butter, softened

½ cup sugar

1 egg

1 teaspoon vanilla extract

½ cup milk

In a bowl, mix flour, cocoa, baking powder, baking soda, and salt. In a separate bowl, cream the butter with sugar. Add egg and vanilla extract to butter mixture. To the butter mixture, alternately add the flour mixture and milk. Begin and end this process with the flour mixture. Spoon into 2-inch cupcake liners, about three-quarters full. Bake at 350 degrees for 12 minutes.

GLAZE

¼ cup heavy cream

1 cup semi-sweet chocolate chips

Nonpareil candies for garnish

Mix the cream and chocolate chips in a small saucepan over low heat until melted and smooth. Remove from heat and ice the cupcakes. Top each cupcake with a nonpareil chocolate candy.

Makes 24 mini cupcakes

TABLE
8

I CAN SEE CLEARLY NOW WITH
TEN PAIRS OF GLASSES

So Slageter

God, grant me the senility to forget the people I never liked anyway, the good fortune to run into the ones I do, and the eyesight to tell the difference.
—**UNKNOWN**

Life begins at forty, but so do fallen arches, rheumatism, faulty eyesight, and the tendency to tell a story to the same person three or four times.
—**HELEN ROWLAND**

You can't depend on your eyes when your imagination is out of focus.
—**MARK TWAIN**

Age shouldn't affect you. You are either marvelous or you are boring, regardless of your age.
—**MORRISSEY**

Older people shouldn't eat health food; they need all the preservatives they can get.
—**ROBERT ORBEN**

The spiritual eyesight improves as the physical eyesight declines.
—**PLATO**

I refuse to think of them as chin hairs. I think of them as stray eyebrows.
—**JANETTE BARBER**

Whatever you may look like, marry a man your own age; as your beauty fades, so will his eyesight.
—**PHYLLIS DILLER**

So Slageter
THE INSPIRATION

One evening while chatting with friends at a party, we divulged that although we love to needlepoint, it had to be solo because these days we can't see the petit point canvas. To remedy this, we decided to start a highly exclusive Stitch and Bitch group with one mandatory requirement. Everyone must be unaffected enough to publicly use reading glasses and oblivious if a seatmate is wearing three pairs. No one even snickers. Even if someone exhumes a large, chest-sitting magnifier with an attached light from her bag of jumbled yarn, the question is "Can I try that?" Outside, in the real world, some of these members are stiletto-strutting socialites, but inside our secret, hallowed sanctuary, we all are replicas of our pictured bespectacled Dolly. So for lunch once a month, we share laughs, news in the hood, and new blogs, books, and Pinterest pins. We just have to sit and listen; our feet don't throb, and we have belts, sandals, dog collars, and Christmas stockings galore to show for it.

- In Babs's New Canaan group, every member is a rotating host and is responsible for supplying the lunch and refreshments. Most times it's a pot of soup, small sandwiches, and dessert. In Dallas, my group always goes to one friend's sunroom filled with natural light.

- To make a needlepoint group absolutely no hassle, some people bring their own lunch or schedule the stitching during late afternoon or cocktail hour.

- Lighting is essential for needlework. As I always tell my clients, "No one is going to sit in that chair if there is no lighting." Buy yourself just one good floor lamp. You will be amazed at how much more you will read and stitch.

- Buy your reading glasses at eyebobs and Costco in bulk.

- Remember, you really only need a group of one to complete your project. Turn on the TV and watch Netflix.

TABLE 9

BEST FRIEND'S LUNCHEON

So Chic

I choose my friends how I like my cocktails . . . strong, fabulous, and with a twist.
—ESTHER BLUM

We never know the true value of friends. While they live, we are too sensitive to their faults. When we have lost them, we only see their virtues.
—JULIUS HARE AND AUGUSTUS HARE

I get by with a little help from my friends.
—JOHN LENNON AND PAUL McCARTNEY

Good friends are like stars—you don't always see them, but you know they're always there.
—CONFUCIUS

Lots of people want to ride with you in the limo, but what you want is someone who will take the bus with you when the limo breaks down.
—OPRAH WINFREY

A true friend is someone who thinks you are a good egg even though he knows that you are slightly cracked.
—BERNARD MELTZER

It takes a long time to grow an old friend.
—JOHN LEONARD

One sure way to lose another woman's friendship is to try to improve her flower arrangements.
—MARCELENE COX

unt Marie was our Irish grandmother's best friend. Oddly enough, she was also her sister-in-law, as they were married to identical twins. Milt and Harry were quite the entertainers. To quote the author, Sister Mary Kathryn (Harry's daughter), in an actual excerpt from our family's genealogy report, "Every week, Milt played the piano and Harry sang at the Cincinnati School for the Deaf." Obviously, our genetics speak for themselves.

Both widowed, Elizabeth and Marie each lived with their children about forty minutes apart. They talked daily, but neither could drive, so they would take turns for week-long visits, composed of boisterous lunches and dinners. You've heard of Margaritaville; well, by week's end, this turned into Manhattanville. Both host families would anticipate the Manhattan weeks because the stories, antics, and laughing never stopped. So go on . . . call a good friend and crank up the blender.

- Once again, use handsome trays for centerpiece groupings, which lends coherence for our dissimilar glasses and vases. Fabulous trays are available in every store at every price range. Try glass, silver, lacquer, marble, wood, or Lucite ones to achieve totally different looks. Here are some great places to find trays: Jonathan Adler, Z Gallerie, Crate & Barrel, Pottery Barn, West Elm, CB2, Olioboard, and Pier 1 Imports, to name a few.

- Keep your eye out for goodies. These gold bow napkin rings were from an antique mall for such little money that we bought all forty-eight. Turned upside down, they double as name card holders.

- Plant flowers and flowering shrubs in your yard because then you will usually have fresh flowers available. I swear we bought our California house mainly because the garden was profuse with lilac and rhododendron bushes. You can even cut posies from small pots kept in a sunroom. Pansies and hyacinths grow perfectly in indoor pots. Nothing brightens an entry hall like a small vase containing the cheery faces of Johnny-jump-ups.

- Have you ever been to Washington, DC, in the spring when the cherry blossom trees are blooming? These tall spring branches are wonderful on the front hall tables for greeting your guests. You can find flowering branches (Bradford pear, forsythia, viburnum) in your yard; many florists also sell them. Clip the desired size branch from the tree. Cut a one- to two-inch slit in the stem so it will take in more water. For large branches, use a vase at least one-third as tall as the stem to prevent it from toppling over. Fill container with lukewarm water and powdered preservative. These usually last about two weeks if you change the water every other day.

- You can find beautiful sets of glasses at the above websites as well as at estate and garage sales, which are usually advertised in the classified section of your local paper on Thursdays and Fridays. Or look online. Also look at auction houses and eBay for amazing bargains on glassware, tableware, and silver. In addition, use glasses or silver julep cups filled with flowers and votive candles to brighten up a naked mantel.

- These pink-and-green tassel plates pictured were found by Babs at Harvey Nichols department store in Knightsbridge. Other good places to find place settings of china are your local department stores and Replacements, Ltd.

- Bring on the high-quality grosgrain, organdy, and satin ribbons. The uses of ribbon are endless: chair backs, chandeliers, and napkin rings, to list a few. We loved a friend's comment that they can decipher the giver of their present just from our wonderful ribbon. Go to Jo-Ann Fabric & Crafts or M&J Trimming (a favorite place to spend the afternoon in New York City).

Menu

WHISKEY SOURS

CAULIFLOWER SOUP

HONEY LEMON
GRILLED CHICKEN

LEMON SQUARES

OUR GRANDMOTHER'S
CUT-OUT SUGAR
COOKIES

WHISKEY SOURS

The first time we remember hearing the whir of the blender was on our First Communion Days (the parents partied too), and it's all been a blur since. We obviously did not grow up in a house of teetotalers. This recipe serves 4, or 2 of our relatives, and it helps to make any party memorable . . . (or not).

1 6-ounce can frozen lemonade

1 lemonade can of water

1 lemonade can of bourbon

1 egg white

2 cups ice

Mix all in blender.

Serves 4 or as above

HONEY LEMON GRILLED CHICKEN

This is a simple crowd pleaser that is very conducive to preparing ahead, leaving you free to attend to that blender. By the way, guys love it too.

4 chicken breasts, boneless and skinless

Salt

Pepper

½ cup olive oil

½ cup lemon juice

2 tablespoons honey

Season chicken breasts on both sides with salt and pepper. Whisk oil, lemon juice, and honey together and pour over chicken. Marinate for at least 1 hour at room temperature. Grill chicken for 7 minutes a side over medium-high heat, then remove to a platter and cover with foil and allow to rest for 1 hour. Slice thin and serve on arugula.

Serves 6

CAULIFLOWER SOUP

This fabulously rich-tasting yet healthy soup I developed while in college, primarily used to combat "The Freshman 15." Now it is equally effective during a possible 5-pound snowstorm. Hold the chocolate chip cookies. Everyone raves, so you won't need to tell them its cumbersome history.

1 onion, chopped

2 tablespoons olive oil

2 16-ounce bags frozen cauliflower

2 32-ounce cartons chicken broth

1 to 2 tablespoons caraway seed

1 teaspoon pepper

1 cup skim milk

Sauté onion in oil. Add all ingredients except milk. Simmer 1 to 2 hours over low heat. Allow to cool, then puree. Once complete, place in soup pot and add skim milk.

NICE ADDITIONS: serve with roasted cauliflower on top; sprinkle with fresh chives and diced cherry tomatoes.

Serves 6

LEMON SQUARES

An old favorite, this version kicks in with a bit more tartness. The combination of sweet and tart complements many dishes. Guaranteed that these treats will disappear.

5 tablespoons butter, softened

1 cup flour

¼ cup powdered sugar

2 eggs, beaten

2 tablespoons flour

¾ cup sugar

Grate rind of 1 lemon

4 tablespoons lemon juice

Mix butter, flour, and powdered sugar. Press into a 7-inch or 8-inch baking dish. Bake at 350 degrees for 20 minutes. Allow to cool. Mix eggs, flour, sugar, lemon rind, and lemon juice. Pour mixture over cooled crust. Bake at 350 degrees for 20 minutes. Sprinkle with powdered sugar.

Makes 18 small squares

OUR GRANDMOTHER'S CUT-OUT SUGAR COOKIES

This is your best friend's lunch, so there can't be too many desserts, right? Beam's delicious cut-out cookies are easy to roll out, cut, and bake, and even easier to eat. These are certainly one of the Slageter sisters' favorites.

1 cup butter, softened

1 cup powdered sugar

1 egg, beaten

1 teaspoon almond extract

½ teaspoon vanilla extract

Cream the above ingredients together.

2½ cups flour

¾ teaspoon baking soda

¾ teaspoon cream of tartar

Separately mix flour, baking soda, and cream of tartar. Combine above mixtures to make dough. Refrigerate 1 hour. Roll out on a floured surface with a floured rolling pin. Cut into shapes. Bake at 375 degrees for 6 to 7 minutes. Allow to cool. Prepare glaze and top the cookies.

GLAZE

2 cups powdered sugar

3 tablespoons or more water (to thin)

1 teaspoon almond extract

1 to 2 drops red food coloring

Mix all.

Makes approximately 60 cookies

TABLE
9

BEST FRIEND'S LUNCHEON, POST-PLASTIC SURGERY

So Slageter

I wish I had a twin so I could know what I'd look like without plastic surgery.
—JOAN RIVERS

Plastic surgeons are always making mountains out of molehills.
—DOLLY PARTON

Plastic surgery is a post-modern veil.
—NAWAL EL SAADAWI

Does plastic surgery exist for dogs yet? . . . because it will soon.
—GILLIAN JACOBS

Plastic surgery is like a big elephant sitting in the Hollywood living room.
—PATRICIA HEATON

I had plastic surgery last week. I cut up my credit cards.
—HENNY YOUNGMAN

She got her looks from her father. He's a plastic surgeon.
—GROUCHO MARX

I was going to have plastic surgery until I noticed the doctor's office was full of portraits by Picasso.
—RITA RUDNER

So Slageter
THE INSPIRATION

Because Sue Sue lives in the Big D (as in Double D), this party has a cosmetic surgery twist. (Oh, now we are going to have to move again.) As a woman living in Dallas, not having a cosmetic procedure is like having errant nose hair or a mustache . . . it's just maintenance. You know people are thinking . . . *Why wouldn't she just lift that (or those)?* Even men go underground (hunting) and show up renewed. One day at an elementary school mothers' luncheon, I began my no-plastic surgery commentary when my new friend admonished me in a whisper that I needed to "stop because every one of these twelve fortyish women have had something done." I prodded, "Except you, right?" To my surprise, she was shaking her head no.

I have to admit, Dallas women do look red-carpet gorgeous even in the grocery store at 7 a.m. Eighteen years later, some of those same women at the table have become my best friends. Just when you are tempted to chuckle at their four-inch eyelash and bee-sting lip decisions, God bless them, they are the first at your sickbed with chicken soup, flowers, and all of the current design magazines. I am just hoping that as we progress in years, my refreshed Barbie friends will still like old Midge.

In contrast, Babs laughs that in New Canaan when she wears lipstick in town during the day, people think that they have missed out on an important birthday lunch. Just for the record, the Slageter secret tip to seeming younger is . . . here it comes . . . wait for it . . . blow-up dolls and costumes. If you act immature, we feel it can buy you a few years. So next time your bestie gets a busty, bring her flowers and all of the current fashion magazines and crank up the blender.

- We like to use place cards with themed names. Who's at this table? Dolly (as in Parton), Miss Texas, Phyllis (as in Diller), Joan (as in Rivers), Heidi, Goldie, Meg . . . you get the idea.

- While you are at it, you'd better order two nurses' uniforms: one for your hubby to join in the fun. Don't forget the high heels and padding in all the right places.

- We have also found that our patients seem to love the idea of a relaxing sponge bath. They actually shriek at the sight of our very professionally labeled VNA (Visiting Nurses Association) bucket containing numerous brushes, sponges, and bubble bath. Always a hit . . . right, Jim and Don?

- Buy those giant pretzel or protein shake containers at Costco or Sam's Club to re-label for the patient's ailment or meds. Oh, and try very hard to only eat two of those enormous pretzels a day. Do as I say, not as I do.

- The nurse outfit is a necessary staple. Like the Chihuahua stuffed animal perched in your purse. Grab an all-white outfit and make the cap with poster paper and ribbon or marker. Or order online at BuyCostumes.com. There are always visiting nurse opportunities for all of your friends' torn rotator cuff and meniscus surgeries. Way better than just flowers . . . right, Jim and Don?

TABLE
10

ONE-ALARM CHILI

So Chic

Chili is much improved by having had a day to contemplate its fate.
—**JOHN STEELE GORDON**

Snow and adolescence are the only problems that disappear if you ignore them long enough.
—**EARL WILSON**

Home is the place where, when you have to go there, they have to take you in.
—**ROBERT FROST**

Part of the success in life is to eat what you like [chili and ice cream] and let the food fight it out inside.
—**MARK TWAIN**

A snowball in the face is surely the perfect beginning to a lasting friendship.
—**MARKUS ZUSAK,** *THE BOOK THIEF*

Cleaning your house while your kids are still growing is like shoveling the walk before it stops snowing.
—**PHYLLIS DILLER**

I would like to find a stew or chili that will give me heartburn immediately instead of at three o'clock in the morning.
—**JOHN BARRYMORE**

Snowmen fall from Heaven unassembled.
—**UNKNOWN**

On the eve of a potential blizzard forecast, the large navy- and white-speckled pot would appear on the stove, a sure sign that Dad would be making his famous chili. After a glorious day of building snow forts and lopsided snowmen, nothing tasted better. The anticipation of the warm dish mounted as we reentered our aromatic kitchen and began to peel wet wool layers from our freezer-burned limbs. Mom would also be preparing her signature snowball dessert, which was Graeter's chocolate chip ice cream balls rolled in coconut, placed in the freezer, and later topped with hot fudge sauce. A lit candle was placed in each, and the celebratory song became:

Happy Snow Day to you.
Happy Snow Day to you.
Hope for NO school tomorrow.
We belong at home too.

Because of these fond memories, we always thought our dad's chili was ready for any cook-off until Babs met Stu Stringfellow, the self-proclaimed Chili Czar. This neighborhood comedian and raconteur challenged her to taste a chili better than his. The ultimate test would be to serve both recipes to a group of New Canaan's brave firefighters. They know their chili in any firehouse. And who wouldn't relish a visit from these dashing, jovial, and courageous men who put their lives on the line daily? And since they don't have a calendar . . .

Both chilis mellowed for a day before the dinner. The lip-smacking third helpings for all, as well as two empty pots, seem testament that although there were compliments all around, Stu's chili was the hero-approved recipe.

- If you would like to make Mom's snowballs, use Cincinnati's best ice cream that was on Oprah's "O Best List" and touted by Bobby Flay. You can order online at the Graeter's website. Tell them two of their Fanbassadors sent you. All of the chip ones are particularly fabulous. Look for this ice cream in your local grocery, as they are really expanding. Kroger always stocks Graeter's. Mmmmmm, giant chips.

Menu

QUESO

LAYERED MEXICAN DIP

GUACAMOLE

PICO DE GALLO

CORN BREAD

STU'S FAMOUS CHILI

BROWNIES

Firefighters are very special in the Slageter sisters' lives, and one of us is even married to a fire commissioner. While growing up, we heard numerous renditions of the story of how our great-grandfather, Lt. William Bocklage, a Cincinnati fireman, gave his life at a four-alarm fire at the Onken factory in 1891. Please remember that the members of your fire department are there 24/7 to protect you. You can show your appreciation and share this dinner with your local fire house.

Any combination of the queso, layered Mexican dip, guacamole, and pico de gallo is also perfect as an appetizer for cocktail parties and game-day tailgates.

QUESO

It did not take a village, but it did take the entire family, to concoct this recipe. This is the result of everybody tweaking.

3 tablespoons butter

4 tablespoons flour

¾ cup skim milk

½ cup chicken broth

1 cup shredded mozzarella cheese

1 cup shredded Monterey Jack cheese with jalapeño

3 tablespoons whipped cream cheese

1 tablespoon olive oil

1 poblano pepper, diced

1 red pepper, diced

1 yellow pepper, diced

In a medium saucepan, melt butter and whisk in flour. Mix milk and chicken broth and then whisk into the flour mixture. Cook until thick. Add all the cheeses and cook until melted, then remove from heat. Heat the oil in a skillet and sauté all the peppers. Add peppers to the cheese mix and return to heat. Pour into a serving bowl and dip away. Serve with nacho-style chips.

You can make this dip days ahead and reheat in the microwave.

Serves 8

LAYERED MEXICAN DIP

This has to be waiting on the counter when the boys fly home from school, on game days, and just because. Any excuse will do. You can prepare and refrigerate this ahead of time.

1 can refried beans

½ cup salsa

1 8-ounce container sour cream

1 package taco seasoning mix

3 avocados, mashed with juice of ½ lime and pinch of salt

2 cups shredded cheddar cheese

2 tomatoes, diced

1 can sliced black olives

¼ cup jalapeño peppers, chopped (from the jar)

1 bunch green onions, chopped

½ cup cilantro, chopped

Mix beans with salsa. Spread in a large serving platter with sides. Mix sour cream and taco mix. Spread over the bean mixture. Layer mashed avocados. Evenly layer the cheese, tomatoes, olives, jalapeño, green onion, and cilantro. Serve with nacho-style chips.

Serves 8

STU'S FAMOUS CHILI

Our guest Chef Stu and "Chief" Inger were just the fire that we needed when entertaining the fire department. We guarantee that your guests will clamor for more of this chili with character.

2½ pounds beef chuck, cubed

1½ pounds pork shoulder or country ribs, cubed

¼ cup canola oil

3 medium onions, chopped

3 garlic cloves, minced

1 28-ounce can diced tomatoes

1 16-ounce can pureed or crushed tomatoes

1 16-ounce can whole tomatoes

1 small can tomato paste

2½ cups water

4 teaspoons mild chili powder

2 tablespoons chili con carne seasoning

1 to 2 tablespoons hot or Mexican chili powder
   (optional for hotter chili)

2 tablespoons cocoa (secret ingredient)

3 teaspoons salt

3 teaspoons oregano

2 teaspoons cumin

In a large skillet, brown the meat in hot oil. Leaving the oil, remove the meat and put into a large pot. Sauté onions and garlic in the same oil; add to meat. Add all remaining ingredients to pot and mix well. Cover pot tightly and cook over low heat for 2 hours or until meat is tender. Best if refrigerated overnight and served the next day. For chili con carne with beans, 2 hours before serving, add 2 27-ounce cans of kidney beans to the pot over a low heat. Stir occasionally without breaking the beans. Serve with tortillas or over rice or alone. Have grated cheddar cheese, chopped Bermuda onions, and sour cream toppings to complement the chili.

Serves 8

GUACAMOLE

3 ripe avocados

2 tablespoons fresh lime juice

1 teaspoon kosher salt

¼ teaspoon cumin

¼ teaspoon coriander

3 tablespoons tomatoes, diced

3 tablespoons onion, diced

2 tablespoons cilantro, diced

2 tablespoons jalapeño peppers, diced (from the jar)

Mash the avocados with lime juice. Add rest of the ingredients. Place in a serving dish. To prevent from turning brown if prepared in advance, place Saran-type wrap over the serving dish. Press down and squeeze out all the air bubbles. Remove wrap to serve.

Serves 8

CORN BREAD

Mmmmmmmmmm! This is a true comfort food.

1 cup corn meal

½ cup flour

2 teaspoons baking powder

½ teaspoon baking soda

½ teaspoon salt

1 small can (6-ounce) sweet white corn, drained

2 eggs, beaten

1½ cups shredded cheddar cheese

⅓ cup honey

1 cup milk mixed with juice of ½ lemon

¼ cup canola oil

Mix all the ingredients. Spray a 7-inch baking pan with PAM. Place the mixture in the pan. Bake at 350 degrees for 25 minutes.

Makes 36 small squares. Serves 8

PICO DE GALLO

OK, "gallo" translates to "rooster" in Spanish. You show me where there is any meat or feathers in this recipe. This light, flavorful, and spicy dish is a refreshing companion to the cheesy and other full-bodied snacks that you serve. It's good on anything.

1 pint cherry tomatoes, diced

1 small onion, diced

¼ cup jalapeño peppers, diced (from the jar)

1 tablespoon lime juice

½ teaspoon kosher salt

Mix and serve in a bowl.

Serves 8

BROWNIES

1 stick butter, melted and set aside

2 eggs

½ cup sugar

1 teaspoon vanilla extract

¾ cup sweet ground cocoa

⅔ cup flour

¼ teaspoon baking powder

¼ teaspoon salt

1 cup semi-sweet chocolate chips

Powdered sugar for garnish

Mix eggs, sugar, and vanilla extract. Stir in cooled butter. Separately mix cocoa, flour, baking powder, salt, and chocolate chips. Mix all ingredients together. Spray an 8-inch baking pan with Baker's Joy and spread the ingredients in the pan. Bake at 350 degrees for 25 minutes. Remove and allow to cool. When cool, sift powdered sugar over brownies.

Divide into 24 brownies, serve, and watch them disappear

NOTE: this entire dinner was specially tested, devoured, and unanimously approved by the members of the New Canaan Fire Company No. 1.

TABLE
10

SEVEN-ALARM
CHILI

So Slageter

You might be a firefighter if your kids are afraid to get in water fights with you.

—UNKNOWN

As a child, my family menu consisted of two choices: take it or leave it.

—BUDDY HACKETT

I wanted to be the first woman to burn her bra, but it would've taken the fire department four days to put it out.

—DOLLY PARTON

When tempted to fight fire with fire, remember that the fire department usually uses water.

—UNKNOWN

If crime fighters fight crime and fire fighters fight fire, what do freedom fighters fight?

—GEORGE CARLIN

If you think it's tough being a firefighter, try being a firefighter's wife.

—UNKNOWN

Hug a firefighter and feel warm all over.

—MARILYN MONROE . . . JUST KIDDING, UNKNOWN

You might be a fireman if you've ever said, "She's hot tonight" and not been talking about a girl.

—ANONYMOUS

So Slageter
THE INSPIRATION

Our first encounter with firemen occurred in Cincinnati when we were about five and seven years old. It was a hot humid summer evening about 5:30 p.m., and our grandmother was preparing dinner. Babs decided she would like a refreshing glass of Pepsi and a Hershey bar for an appetizer. Our grandmother was not a fan of the appetizer concept. She subscribed to the clean-your-plate supper concept and told Babs no. For just a second, Grandmother left the chicken frying and the potatoes boiling while she emptied the garbage pail outside. In that instant, Babs saw a solution to her snack dilemma and locked the door behind her warden. Even as a seven-year-old, I knew dinner was going to be late.

Grandmother frantically ran next door to call the fire department, and in minutes, my friend Diane and I were sharing our backyard with hordes of curious neighbors lured by the speeding fire trucks and pealing sirens. (Hairy Mr. Weeks should have really grabbed a shirt, as it's still a bad visual.)

Anyway, as the crowd anxiously stared at our house, all eyes eventually zeroed onto a second floor window where a little cherub was displayed proudly by a smiling fireman. She was drinking a Pepsi, and he was eating a Hershey bar.

5:55 p.m. Hi Mom and Dad; welcome home!

- For the table decorations, we gathered everything that was heat related: fire extinguishers, every hot sauce, "damper open" needlepoint sign, duct tape painted on fire from the hardware store, toy fire engines, loving-trophy cups filled with red hot gumballs, and of course, boxes of Hot Tamales candy.

- Because we invited firemen, we thought that it would be insensitive to have real fire on the table. We ordered battery-operated flicker candles; get them from Pier 1 Imports, Pottery Barn, or Home Depot.

- These candles will be used over and over. Having a party? Place on mantels or around the pool or yard for a stunning appearance. Don't forget to buy batteries in bulk.

- The firemen at our dinner were too modest to comment, but we spelled out our appreciation of these dauntless men by making chair-back decorations. Attributes such as Brave, Daring, and Fearless were printed on poster board. To these we added badges from the fireman party favor section of Party City and paired with regimental striped ribbon from our local craft store.

- Trophies made of plastic from Oriental Trading were filled with red Hot Tamales, gumballs, and the flowers, red carnations.

- Sheets of gold and red Mylar were positioned to show through the crack between the door to mimic fire (kind of).

- This is also the time to showcase your American flags and books of bravery, such as *Brave Men*. By the way, books are a great tool to lift otherwise unseen objects. (Also, try using books under a diminutive lamp to give added height.)

TABLE

11

POOLSIDE PARTY

So Chic

Some of the best memories are made in flip flops.
—**Kellie Elmore**

The two best times to keep your mouth shut are when you are swimming and when you are angry.
—**Unknown**

Summer afternoon: to me those have always been the two most beautiful words in the English language.
—**Henry James**

Chlorine is my perfume.
—**Unknown**

It's a good idea to begin at the bottom in everything except learning to swim.
—**Unknown**

One must maintain a little bit of summer, even in the middle of winter.
—**Henry David Thoreau**

Sorry, but it struck me as weird that you were in the pool for hours without leaving to go to the bathroom. I'll remember that.
—**Me to a nine-year-old guest**

If you're not barefoot, you're overdressed.
—**Unknown**

So Chic
THE INSPIRATION

The Slageter family did not have a swimming pool in our backyard, but we did host a pool party. Yes, you have read that correctly. We concocted a *hysterical* plan to reveal to our friends that our parents had installed a swimming pool. We hand delivered the colorful, beach ball invitations. Next the lawn was elaborately decorated. Paper lanterns, strands of white lights, tiki torches, wrought-iron cushioned lounge chairs lugged from the porch, three beautifully set daisy-laden tables, and buckets of refreshments were all strategically placed. In a far corner, we proudly constructed a water park feature, the rotating sprinkler. Tanning in the kiddie pool was already a female family tradition in the Slageters' yard. So for the party, we just added three additional pools—maximum capacity four adults—filled to the brim with refreshing H_2O.

Our fourteen guests eagerly entered the front door carrying their rafts and inner tubes, ready for the big reveal and perhaps a showy dive off the high board. At that moment, we realized that in reality maybe this was not as amusing as we had anticipated. After the initial shock, our good-sport buddies eventually forgave us and slowly began to appreciate our detailed efforts. On a stifling hot August night, everyone came to realize that it was possible to cool off and have countless belly laughs in just two feet of water.

- Inexpensive hot pink cloth napkins are from Hobby Lobby.

- White ruffled flower container is from Pier 1 Imports.

- Chippendale white chair place card holders (Christmas ornaments) are from Pier 1 Imports.

- Chair cushion fabric is from Scalamandré, through an interior decorator.

- White topiaries are from Two's Company or One Kings Lane.

- Monogrammed bath sheet towels are from Leontine Linens.

- Hot pink paper placemats are from Needle in a Haystack. Lots of stationary stores carry these.

- Plastic glassware is a must poolside, available even at the grocery store.

- White-and-pink tray is from Z Gallerie.

- Paper lanterns, strings of lights, and tiki torches are well stocked at Pier 1 Imports, Pottery Barn, and Target. Stock up at end-of-season sales.

Menu

FROZEN DAIQUIRIS

MARINATED
FLANK STEAK

ORZO SALAD

CORN PUDDING

STRAWBERRY PIE

RECIPES

FROZEN DAIQUIRIS

This will get your party started with a big splash.

1 12-ounce can frozen lemonade

1 6-ounce can frozen limeade

1 bottle rum

3 lemonade cans of water

Mix all and freeze.

Serves 12

MARINATED FLANK STEAK

Many marinated flank steak recipes contain too much oil. I came up with this marinade using just ingredients that most people have on hand.

1½ pounds flank steak

¼ cup soy sauce, lite

1 tablespoon sesame oil

1 tablespoon hoisin sauce

½ tablespoon honey

1½ teaspoons ginger flakes

Trim excess fat from the flank steak. Put the steak in a Pyrex dish large enough to accommodate the steak. Mix the soy sauce, sesame oil, hoisin sauce, honey, and ginger. Pour over the steak. Marinate at room temperature for 2 hours, turning the steak 1 or 2 times to help marinate both sides. Grill over high heat 5 minutes per side. Let it rest for 5 minutes or so before slicing.

Serves 6

CORN PUDDING

Very summertime and terrific with steak. You can use fresh corn, but I find that the canned corn has the same great taste.

2 12-ounce cans sweet corn, drained

2 eggs, beaten

½ cup light cream

¾ cup chicken broth

½ cup cheddar cheese, shredded

1 cup Monterey Jack cheese, cubed

Mix all ingredients together. Bake in a 1½- to 2-quart casserole sprayed with PAM at 375 degrees for 1 hour. Let stand for 10 to 15 minutes before serving.

Serves 6

ORZO SALAD

1½ cups orzo, cooked and drained

1 large red pepper, diced

1 red onion, diced

6 cloves garlic, sliced

1 tablespoon olive oil

1 teaspoon salt

1 teaspoon pepper

8 slices of bacon, cooked, drained and crumbled

2 ounces crumbled goat cheese

½ cup chopped basil

½ cup roasted nuts

Cook orzo. Drain.

Mix red pepper, onion, garlic, oil, salt, and pepper. Roast in a 400-degree oven for 20 minutes. Combine all ingredients. Cool and serve.

Serves 6

STRAWBERRY PIE

A refreshing, light summer dessert that disappears as quickly as you serve it.

GRAHAM CRACKER CRUST

1 cup graham cracker crumbs

2 tablespoons melted butter

2 tablespoons sugar

Mix ingredients. Pat into a pie plate. Bake at 350 degrees for 8 to 10 minutes.

STRAWBERRY FILLING

1 cup water

¼ cup sugar

2 tablespoons cornstarch

3 tablespoons strawberry gelatin mix

1 quart fresh strawberries, washed, sliced thin, and layered in the crust

In a saucepan, cook the water, sugar, and cornstarch over medium-high heat for 5 minutes or until thick. Add gelatin mix. Mix and pour over the strawberries. Allow pie to cool.

TOPPING

1 8-ounce carton whipping cream

1 tablespoon powdered sugar

Whip the cream. Add sugar and mix. Spoon over the pie. Sift powdered sugar over the pie.

Serves 6

TABLE

11

THE EDMONDSON
SWIM CLUB

So Slageter

I refuse to join any club that would have me as a member.
—**GROUCHO MARX**

Beginner's Swim Class: 9:00–10:00 Memorial for Drowning Victims: 10:00–11:00
—**UNKNOWN**

The bowling alley is the poor man's country club.
—**SANFORD HANSELL**

My wife made me join a bridge club. I jump off next Tuesday.
—**RODNEY DANGERFIELD**

At the beach, a guy was swimming in the ocean, yelling, "Help! Shark!" I just laughed; I knew that shark was not going to help him.
—**UNKNOWN**

If one synchronized swimmer drowns, do all the rest have to drown too?
—**UNKNOWN**

If swimming is so good for the figure, how do you explain whales?
—**CHARLES SAATCHI**

Swim at your own risk—lifeguard at happy hour.
—**UNKNOWN**

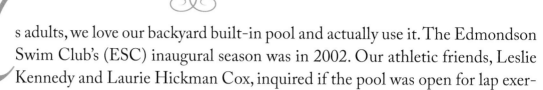

So Slageter
THE INSPIRATION

As adults, we love our backyard built-in pool and actually use it. The Edmondson Swim Club's (ESC) inaugural season was in 2002. Our athletic friends, Leslie Kennedy and Laurie Hickman Cox, inquired if the pool was open for lap exercises. Since one mile in our compact pool equals 356 laps, I felt safe allowing lap swimming. To emulate other clubs in the area (as in country), it was decided by the management (me) to request an application from all names on the waiting list (two). After one is approved by the management committee (me), one receives the official laminated club pass, which must be shown to the management (me) each time before entering the club and worn at all times while on the premises. There are three membership levels. It is wise to seriously consider the platinum level as the perks are a flowered swim cap with a flattering chin strap and free water bottle.

While slathered with SPF 50 and floating on a Styrofoam noodle, desperate cellulite dilemma and embarrassing moments are open for discussion. Special theme days (Beauty Contest) have been well received by the membership (six). Just like our pageant sisters, we strut in bathing suits, wearing high heels and suntan panty hose. (Find these dinosaurs on the back row of any drugstore, next to the Depends.) For the talent portion of synchronized swimming, flowered bathing caps are added.

The management has exciting plans for upcoming seasons, reciprocal club visits. Here's how it works:

1. The management will learn the vacation schedules of other friends with nice big pools.

2. The management will coerce the friendly housekeepers into letting ESC members in for a sly dip.

3. After the fact, the management will send postcards to the vacationers showing ESC members on our new (bought with initiation fees) giant swan float, holding a sign saying, "Wish you were here!"

The management anticipates a hefty waiting list with this exciting news.

As you can surmise, club life is a quirky and low-key way to connect with close friends in the summertime when the living is easy. So once again, crank up that blender and call the members.

- After the membership card is filled out, laminate for protection. You don't have a laminating machine? No problem. The management has found that the new members enjoy coming in the office to watch the process. You need a roll of clear tape and dexterity. Tape the card in consecutive rows on front and back, then trim with scissors. Now make a hole with punch, thread some yarn, and the card is ready for the season.

- A lifeguard is a necessity at any club, including ours. As you can see, all that you need is a step-ladder and a counter stool from your kitchen to construct the stand. Unfortunately, Dolly is reading her current tabloids for inquiring minds, so she can't blow her whistle and yell, "Sharks!" to alert members of impending danger. Shark hats are from Oriental Trading.

- Don't forget to load up on the bottled water as promised in the contract. The management has been caught refilling discarded bottles, which was met with disfavor.

- Flowered swim caps with chin straps can be found at AllSwim.com.

- Appoint one of the members as the Club Director. It will be her responsibility to get the water.

EDMONDSON SWIM CLUB MEMBER

Name _____
Address _____
Soc Sec # _____
Bank Acc# _____
Next of Kin _____
X _____
Exp _____

Edmondson Swim Club

, **Platinum Member-** Towel ,monogrammed noodle and bottled water provided

, **Gold Member-** Towel and bottled water provided

, **Silver Member-** Bring your own damn stuff

Please read and sign agreement:
I promise that I will go to restroom in the backhouse.

X_____ date_____

Management has the right to remove any member who inebriated, incontinent or in need of electrolysis.

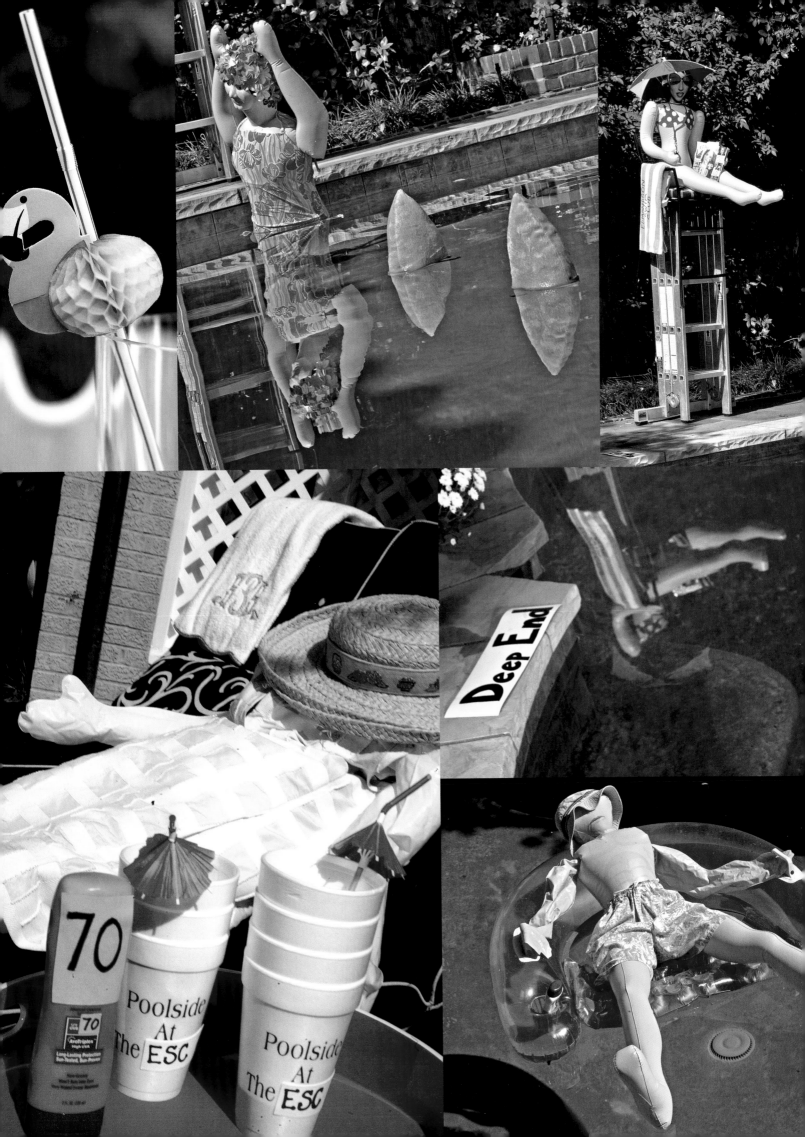

BABS AND SUE SUE'S INDISPENSABLE
APPENDIX OF SHOPPING FUN

Here is a list of some of our favorite haunts, where we get our supplies, along with their Web addresses and why we love them. Some are mentioned in the book, and some are not. But you can't go wrong with any of these businesses.

ABOUT.COM

www.About.com

Learn how to needlepoint the basket-weave stitch all by your own self.

ALLPOSTERS.COM

www.AllPosters.com

We love the cardboard celebrity life-size cutouts to greet our guests. You know it's going to be a stupendous swim party when David Hasselhoff and Pamela Anderson are your initial sightings at the front door.

ALLSWIM.COM

www.AllSwim.com

Who doesn't look stunning in a flowered swim cap with chin strap? Instant jaw lift! This is the platinum-level incentive if joining our swim club.

AMAZON

www.Amazon.com

Here's where we got some of our glittered Santas for the Yuletide Brunch and some of the white compotes . . . along with everything else under the sun.

ANTHROPOLOGIE

www.Anthropologie.com

Unlikely but interesting tabletop finds and even where we found some of our holiday items.

ARCHIE MCPHEE

www.ArchieMcPhee.com

If you need a Best Dog trophy, a wind-up Nunzilla, or a lederhosen-wearing unicorn—and who doesn't?—this is your spot.

BBJ

www.BBJLinen.com

Don't load the washer and dryer. Rent your tablecloths and napkins.

BIZRATE

www.Bizrate.com

Need Eiffel towers?

BLUE PRINT

BluePrintStore.com

Lovely designer's store in a restored home. Sure to inspire.

BUYCOSTUMES.COM

www.BuyCostumes.com

We are on a first-name basis at this shop. They have nurse outfits, gorilla hands, big plastic derrières, and hundreds of outlandish wigs. So many choices, so little time.

CAFÉ DU MONDE

CafeDuMonde.com

Order your strong coffee and beignets for brunch directly from the French Quarter. Maybe they will even throw in something for that headache.

CANDY DIRECT

www.CandyDirect.com

This site even has candy by color. Perfect for making our candy trees.

CARDBOARD CUTOUTS

www.CardboardCutouts.com

Yes, we like stand-ups for everyday use. Austin Powers loved riding in the carpool line, and Xena the Warrior Princess frequented the high school football pep rallies.

CARTWRIGHT'S SEQUINS

www.CCartwright.com

Before you make your Olympic ice skating costume, go here to buy your sequins and beads in bulk. You can also get these sequins in thousands of different colors to make our Christmas tree skirts.

CB2

www.CB2.com

Reasonably priced trays, glasses, and tabletop items.

CONSIDER THE COOK

www.ConsiderTheCook.com

New Canaan's first stop for all things for the kitchen.

THE CONTAINER STORE

www.ContainerStore.com

If you are working on the tree skirts, this should be your first stop for buying compartmentalized boxes before you ever think about ordering the sequins and beads. If you ignore this directive, your room will resemble Sixth Avenue the day after the Macy's Thanksgiving Day Parade. Not kidding.

COOPER OAKS DESIGN

CooperOaksDesign.com

Unique needlepoint canvases with beach, floral, ranch, and Nantucket basket themes.

COQUEREL FAMILY WINE ESTATES

www.CoquerelWines.com

Proprietors Brenda and Clay Cockerell take pride in these excellent wines from Napa Valley.

COSTCO

www.Costco.com

Stock up on reading glasses in bulk and giant plastic pretzel containers to keep the Viagra and Vicodin in.

THE COTTAGE SHOP

www.TheCottageShop.com

For the Francophile, this site is Limoges box heaven.

CRATE & BARREL

www.CrateAndBarrel.com

We like the Cartier-like rolling napkin rings and aqua milk glass plates for our Thirtieth Anniversary, Wedded Bliss.

CREATIVE STITCHES AND GIFTS

CreativeStitchesAndGifts.com

A Dallas needlepoint store that also offers classes.

CustomTshirts

www.CustomTshirts.com

Print anything for your theme, such as our Dad's Swinging Half-Century, No-Women-Allowed Club gathering. Please don't make one that says, "I'm with Stupid." That would be understood.

DAVID AUSTIN ROSES

www.DavidAustinRoses.com

Our mom loved these roses in her garden.

eBAY

www.EBay.com

This is the only site to search for plastic blow-up dolls. Trust us on this one.

ELLIS HILL

www.Ellis-Hill.com

This is an upscale boutique with one-of-a-kind monogrammed stationery and gifts. Order some monogrammed linen placemats for the anniversary party: "Happy Anniversary, Honey!" These owners are fun friends with the most exquisite taste.

ETSY

www.Etsy.com

Here's a treasure trove of white and gold dishes for your French party.

EYEBOBS

www.Eyebobs.com

This site has fashionable reading glasses sure to bring compliments. Even though you can't see squat, you'll look cool and smart from the other end.

THE FIND

www.TheFind.com

A great source for china as well as white and gold compotes.

FORTY FIVE TEN

www.FortyFiveTen.com

This store has beautiful, one-of-a-kind designer objects to wow your party guests.

GAMBINO'S BAKERY

www.Gambinos.com

The king of king cakes in New Orleans. Order one to end the mystery of "What's a king cake?"

GRAETER'S

www.Graeters.com

The best ice cream in the world, with humongous chocolate chips. On Oprah's list . . . and on our thighs.

HARRODS

www.Harrods.com

London's premiere department store, whose sales are legendary. We love our beautiful crystal stemware and decanters.

HAYDEL'S BAKERY

www.HaydelBakery.com

Another great option for king cakes during Carnival.

HARVEY NICHOLS

www.HarveyNichols.com

Another great London shop where Babs nabbed our coveted pink tassel plates used in our Best Friend's Luncheon.

HERMÈS

www.Hermes.com

Luckily the boys have started using this shop to get the enamel bracelets, scarves, and leather goods for big-occasion gift giving. Let's just say they have figured out that this guarantees some home cooking and less talking.

HOBBY LOBBY

www.HobbyLobby.com

Stock up on Styrofoam Christmas tree forms for applying candy, gold plastic chargers for the Knights of the Round Table from the Swinging Half Century Club, and colorful polka dot napkins to use poolside. Now get out of there quickly before you end up buying a Bedazzler kit.

HOME DEPOT

www.HomeDepot.com

Get some battery-powered flickering candles as well as pink light bulbs for the romantic ambiance at the Thirtieth Anniversary, Wedded Bliss ideas. This is the only place on this list that hubby will gladly accompany you.

HOUSE OF NEEDLEPOINT

HouseOfNeedlepoint.com

This store has needlepoint classes and is a favorite in Darien, Connecticut.

JINGLENOG

JingleNog.com

Economical and cute Christmas ornaments for bowls during holiday gatherings.

JO-ANN FABRIC AND CRAFT STORES

www.Joann.com

A sure bet for all of your fabric and trim needs. Get the felt for tree skirts as well as red and white fabric for no-sew Christmas chair backs and the knight tunics.

JONATHAN ADLER

www.JonathanAdler.com

Current stylish trays and accessories.

KATE SPADE

www.KateSpade.com

We love to dress Dolly and each other in Kate Spade frocks.

KROGER

www.Kroger.com

Buy your Graeter's coconut or mocha chocolate chip ice cream here on your way home from Pilates.

Leontine Linens

www.LeontineLinens.com

New Orleans store with elegant monogrammed linens and placemats.

Lyrics.com

www.Lyrics.com

We use this resource repeatedly to make custom lyrics for birthday songs: "Pretty Woman," "Rhinestone Cowboy," "Home on the Range," "How Do You Solve a Problem Like Maria," "Wild Thing," and "I Can't Help Myself (Sugar Pie, Honey Bunch)" have all been rewritten and karaoked. Be sure and print out lots of copies for all to join in the roast.

M&J Trimming

www.MJTrim.com

We would love to be accidentally locked in overnight at this colossal ribbon and trim store in New York City.

M's Canvashouse

www.MsCanvashouse.com

This Kentucky store has a wonderful selection of needlepoint belts, canvases, and ornaments.

Madison 214

Madison214.com

Everyone's go-to shop in Highland Park Village for fabulous linens, china, and gifts, all beautifully gift wrapped in their signature navy-and-white thick grosgrain ribbon. Ahhhh . . . perfection is in the details.

The Maids of DuPage County

TheMaidsOfDuPageCounty.com

Make this your first call if you decide to have a party for your nine-year-old son despite our advice.

MardiGrasOutlet.com

www.MardiGrasOutlet.com

Order your ten thousand Mardi Gras beads and trinkets. Just remember that you won't be able to get rid of these fast enough on Ash Wednesday. Just saying.

Michaels

www.Michaels.com

Don't forget to buy your poster board, glue guns, glue sticks, ribbon, royal crowns, and throne paint for your next royal victim.

Needle in a Haystack

www.NeedleStack.com

Family-owned store full of tasteful paper goods, invitations, and friendly advice.

Needlepoint For Fun

www.Needlepoint-For-Fun.com

Want to have a rip-roaring Saturday night? Watch needlepoint tutorial videos.

Needlepoint This!

NeedlepointThis.com

Dallas needlepoint store that also offers classes.

Neiman Marcus

www.NeimanMarcus.com

The best of everything, anywhere. We adore the first-class service by the incomparable and affable staff. If you are ever in Dallas, you owe it to yourself to visit this flagship legend. Have at least one of Chef Kevin Garvin's signature popovers in the Zodiac Room. China, silver, glassware, and our L'Objet pagoda salt and peppers are just a fraction of all of the things that should be on your wish list.

Nest

www.NestDallas.com

This is a terrific gift store with a cutting-edge vibe.

Olioboard

Olioboard.com

Go to this site for an abundance of trays, china, and gifts.

One Kings Lane

www.OneKingsLane.com

Fill your whole house through this website. We bought the poolside party white ceramic topiaries while browsing their website at 1:00 a.m.

Oriental Trading

www.OrientalTrading.com

This site has been a party source for ages. Wigs, trophies, colossal fake jewelry, and fireman badges are just a few of the items that constantly tempt us.

Party City

www.PartyCity.com

Plenty of balloons, wigs, swords, and fireman paraphernalia. What's not to love?

Penzeys Spices

www.Penzeys.com

Babs loves these spices and uses Fox Point Seasoning every time she roasts chicken breasts.

Pier 1 Imports

www.Pier1.com

Flickering votive candles with batteries, unusual napkin rings, and lacquer trays are a few of our favorites here. The ruffled planter and Chippendale place card holders (actually in the ornament section) for our Poolside Party were also from here.

Pottery Barn

www.PotteryBarn.com

We cannot get enough of their quality party merchandise such as lanterns, strands of outdoor lights, wicker baskets, trays, and holiday-themed goods.

Rebecca Wood Designs

RebeccaWoodDesigns.com

Browse this outstanding needlepoint site. After ordering your Christmas stocking or ornaments, Pinterest won't be the only thing keeping you up till the wee hours.

Replacements, Ltd.

www.Replacements.com

They say, "We replace the irreplaceable!" So you found your Francis the First sterling silver fork in the sandbox? Better replace it now, as you will need one for your anniversary dinner, unless you are the trophy wife; then you can just buy twenty-four new place settings of Buccellati from Neiman's.

Scully & Scully

www.ScullyAndScully.com

Race to Park Avenue in New York City to buy one of the Christmas Hospitality trees, as seen on our Yuletide Brunch table. We love the incorporation of old-world Florentine paper on these glittered beauties.

St. Michael's Woman's Exchange

St-Michaels-Womans-Exchange.com

We love to support lovely gift stores like this (all over the country). The staff are darling volunteers who are always cheerful and knowledgeable.

Stanley Korshak

www.StanleyKorshak.com

Beautiful family-owned store with a luxurious gift department. The sales people are amazing.

Stupid.com

www.Stupid.com

Of course, we flip over this goofy gag site. Where else can you buy squirrel underpants, mustaches, and tattoo sleeves? We own them all. Without this stuff, life could be so boring.

Tapley Entertainment

www.LookAlike.com

We booked Austin Powers for a going-away party when our friend Emma was moving back to England. Much to our dismay, mid-conga line, ample Austin doffed his shirt to reveal a fake carpet of chest and back hair. We are all still laughing/crying ten years later. If that's appalling to you, there is always the SNL Church Lady.

Target

www.Target.com

Loading up that basket with paper towels and cases of water? Go ahead and cruise down the tabletop aisle. This is where we got those zippy black-and-white dessert plates for Dad's party, outside paper lanterns, and—shhhh—some Spanx.

Two's Company

www.TwosCompany.com

Peruse this site for innovative, colorful products and diversely fun themes. Our rhinestone picture frames for the trophy wives showing off their new faces were found here, as well as some fabulous boxwood topiaries.

Vintage Living

LisaLubyRyan.com

This friend's shop has handpicked French tableware, artifacts, and all things Christmas.

Wayside Gardens

www.WaysideGardens.com

Order this catalog if only to drool over the perfect garden. Then order viburnum and lilac bushes for your yard so that you can always have posies on your front hall table (at least in the spring).

West Elm

www.WestElm.com

Plenty of trays, glasses, and plates, fairly priced.

The Whitney Shop

TheWhitneyShop.com

Connecticut brides register here for life keepsakes and good advice from the wonderful women on staff.

Wisteria

www.Wisteria.com

Their catalog is filled with striking items for any party theme. Look for their sale merchandise.

YouTube

www.YouTube.com

Focus, focus. Remember, you are on YouTube to learn how to needlepoint.

Z Gallerie

www.ZGallerie.com

Inexpensive fun items to give your table pizzazz. Here is another place to grab a leather or lacquer tray.

Zurchers

www.Zurchers.com

Uh oh . . . silly string! We love the large paper globes, pastel-colored rock candy to bring to your dentist, and bang-for-the-buck tassel garlands.

ABOUT THE
AUTHORS

The nuns would not approve of any bragging, but...

Babs Horner is a gourmet caterer of Absolutely Babulous and a needlepoint entrepreneur with It's a Stitch. She lives with her husband Jack in New Canaan, Connecticut, and has two daughters.

Susan "Sue Sue" Palma is a nationally and locally published decorator, owner of Susan Palma Interiors and co-owner of The Design Girls with Muffin Lemak. She lives in Dallas, Texas, with her husband Gene and has two sons.

The sisters are not socialites, but instead call themselves *faux*cialites who have planned and directed numerous charity events. These have included galas, a luncheon for one thousand, a black-tie comedy night, Festival of Trees and Deck the Hall seasonal events, various school carnivals, and auctions from coast to coast. Both have been lucky to have had repeat clients for twenty-five years.

In addition, they are both addicted to Pinterest and are proud members of the clubs Fruit of the Month, Costco, and the Edmondson Swim Club.

If you are *really* clamoring for more information, please visit www.SophisticationIsOverrated.com.